Japanese gardening

Japanese gardening

An inspirational guide to designing and creating an authentic

Japanese garden with over 260 exquisite photographs

Charles Chesshire

Photography by Alex Ramsay

This edition is published by Aquamarine, an imprint of Anness Publishing Ltd, Hermes House, 88–89 Blackfriars Road, London SE1 8HA; tel. 020 7401 2077; fax 020 7633 949

www.aquamarinebooks.com; www.annesspublishing.com

If you like the images in this book and would like to investigate using them for publishing, promotions or advertising, please visit our website www.practicalpictures.com for more information.

UK agent: The Manning Partnership Ltd; tel. 01225 478444; fax 01225 478440; sales@manning-partnership.co.uk

UK distributor: Grantham Book Services Ltd; tel. 01476 541080; fax 01476 541061; orders@gbs.tbs-ltd.co.uk

North American agent/distributor: National Book Network; tel. 301 459 3366; fax 301 429 5746; www.nbnbooks.com

Australian agent/distributor: Pan Macmillan Australia; tel. 1300 135 113; fax 1300 135 103; customer.service@macmillan.com.au

New Zealand agent/distributor: David Bateman Ltd; tel. (09) 415 7664; fax (09) 415 8892

Publisher Joanna Lorenz; **Editorial Director** Judith Simons
Executive Editor Caroline Davison; **Editor** Emma Clegg
Photographer Alex Ramsay; **Additional Photography** Peter Anderson, Jonathan Buckley and Steven Wooster; **Designer** Simon Daley
Illustrator Anna Koska; **Production Controller** Wendy Lawson

With thanks to Nao Yano and Misako Lodge for their helpful translations.

ETHICAL TRADING POLICY

Because of our ongoing ecological investment programme, you, as our customer, can have the pleasure and reassurance of knowing that a tree is being cultivated on your behalf to naturally replace the materials used to make the book you are holding. For further information, please go to www.annesspublishing.com/trees

Page 1: The entrance to the temple garden of Koto-in, Kyoto, shows the dramatic interplay between architecture and the natural forms of trees and moss against a background of bamboo forest.

Page 2: The soaring trunks of Japanese cedars (Cryptomeria japonica), break out of carpets of moss at Sanzen-in, Ohara.

Page 3: A stone pagoda stands in a grove of the rare Chinese fir (Cunninghamia lanceolata) in the stroll garden of Syoko-ho-en, Kyoto.

Above from left to right: A tea house at Saiho-ji Moss Temple in Kyoto; Chinese-style wooden bridge; geometric entrance pathway at Koetsu-ji.

Opposite from left to right: The garden of Isui-en "borrows" the view of a neighbouring temple; Japanese koi carp; a gateway along a tea path.

Contents

Introduction

The Japanese garden has captured the imagination of Western gardeners for many years. Japan, isolated from the rest of the world from the 1630s for over 200 years, had been nurturing extraordinary and unique styles of architecture, poetry, painting, flower arranging and gardening. When artists, architects and designers in the West were exposed to these Japanese arts in the late 19th century, they were astonished by what they found.

The strong influence of the Japanese arts is still being felt today. Of these arts, the Japanese garden, in particular, holds a powerful and mystical grip. Steeped in significance and refinement, the Japanese garden has enormous appeal, especially for garden designers seeking a deeper meaning and a more contemporary edge for their own gardens.

Japanese landscape gardens, especially those constructed of stone and sand (some as long ago as the 1400s), have become the benchmark of abstract garden art throughout the world. It was the dynamic, creative energies of the Zen monks and painters of the medieval period that set the stage for the development of the exceptional art form that is the Japanese garden.

Plants are fundamental to all but a few Japanese gardens, with gardeners celebrating the seasons through the fleeting beauty of the plants. Most of those that have earned a place in the gardens of the Japanese possess poetic significance, whether it is the twisted pine, the scattered cherry blossom, the pendulous wisteria, the symbolic lotus or the fiery autumn maple. These plants are always placed, as with each rock or lantern, with restraint and care. Everything in the Japanese garden serves a role in the creation of a unified, harmonious and poetic picture. This gardening culture is an art in which the result is far greater than the sum of its parts.

Right A Japanese white pine (*Pinus parviflora*), possibly over 700 years old, is the main feature of the garden at Hosen-in. The veranda pillars frame the scene, their upright form echoing the poles supporting the pine.

The history of the Japanese garden

The evolution of this gardening tradition is both long and fascinating. Understanding its history and the people involved in it will provide an insight into the philosophy that inspires the Japanese garden as well as an ability to create gardens in this style with confidence and conviction. Although the style of Japanese gardens can be imitated simply by copying their outward form and appearance, it requires a much deeper understanding of these gardens to reproduce their spirit. Wave after wave of Chinese and Buddhist influences over the centuries have combined with the Japanese strong sense of self, as well as their glorious natural landscape and native religion, to produce the uniquely curious, distinctive and beautiful art form that is the Japanese garden.

Opposite The dry garden at the temple of Ryogen-in, Kyoto, was redesigned in 1980 using the theme of the legends of the Mystic Isles.

Above, from left Moss and square pavers, a stone lantern, and clipped azaleas: all the work of designer Mirei Shigemori in the 1930s at Tofuku-ji.

The Japanese garden as we know it is the result of various creative influences, starting with the Chinese myths of the Mystic Isles, the islands of the immortals, who in the Heian period were believed to possess the elixir of eternal youth. When Japanese gardeners first encountered Chinese gardens, it was this cult of immortality that engrossed them. Mountains, islands and lakes were central to these garden paradises and later became enduring symbols for Buddhists as well. Another important influence is a respect for nature, rooted in Japan's native Shinto religion, which gave energy and life to rocks and trees, and a passion for plants and their symbolic poetry.

At significant moments in their long history, the Japanese have turned to their neighbours across the sea, the Chinese and Koreans, for ways of developing their arts and philosophies. Japanese Buddhist monks made pilgrimages to China to return with Zen, tea, and a reverence for the wisdom of Chinese sages, painters and hermit poets. In the 15th century, the Japanese arts of poetry, theatre and painting, coupled with a devotion to tea and Zen, created the chemistry for the origins of two of Japan's most important garden styles: the dry garden and the tea garden. All gardens subsequent to this period return for inspiration to these two styles, as well as to the romanticism of the Heian Period (AD 785–1184). Time and time again motifs from Heian romanticism, dry gardens and tea gardens re-appear, even in the most avant-garde gardens.

Above, from left A mossy isle in a sea of sand at Tofuku-ji; the stream garden around the temple of Motsu-ji; the classic ingredients of a dry garden, using beach stones, gravel, boulders and granite setts.

Opposite A unique garden shelter called the *ryu-ten* ("teashop in the garden") in the stroll garden of Koraku-en, in Okayama. A stream is channelled through the building, flowing around perfectly set rocks.

The six important periods

There are six important periods in the evolution of the Japanese garden, most coinciding with dramatic changes in Japan's history. The key features of each period – the Nara period, the Heian period, the Kamakura period, the Muromachi period, the Momoyama period and the Edo period – are explained here.

Nara period (AD712–94)

(Chinese Tang dynasty, AD618–906)

A period of pond and stream gardens, and gardens for ceremonies.
Nara, some 48km (30 miles) south of Kyoto, was the last of the ancient capitals of Japan. Excavations made in 1974 found vestiges of a garden on the site of an old palace and revealed a winding stream garden with unique, sophisticated rock arrangements. These gardens were almost certainly used for ceremonial purposes, and were quite similar to those found in China at that time.

Heian period (AD785–1184)

(Chinese Tang dynasty, AD618–906; Five Dynasties, AD906–60; Chinese Song dynasty, AD960–1279)

The first wave of Chinese influence and Pure Land Paradise gardens.
The most romantic period in Japanese cultural history saw many refinements and a new sensitivity to detail, the seasons and rituals evolving under imperial rule in Kyoto. One key feature was the creation of pond and island gardens that incorporated the Mystic Isles of the Immortals and the Pure Land Paradise garden of Buddha Amida, into which the souls of the pure could be reborn. Another was the design of gardens so that court ceremonies, music and poetry readings could be performed in courtyards, on boats, and by the side of streams. The *Sakuteiki*, possibly the world's first great garden treatise, was written in the 11th century.

Kamakura period (1185–1392)

(Chinese Song dynasty, AD960–1279; Yuan or Mongol dynasty, 1279–1368)

The second wave of Chinese influence with the arrival of Zen.
Minamoto was the first shogun and his government, based in Kamakura, took little interest in the arts until Buddhist monks began returning from China with Zen, tea, paintings of the Song dynasty, and early artefacts of the Ming dynasty. The imperial family in Kyoto continued in much the same way as in the Heian period. Around 1339, the Saiho-ji and Tenryu-ji gardens were created in Kyoto, inspired by scenes from Song-dynasty paintings. Rocks were used in greater quantities than before and Zen monks started to make gardens.

Left The Golden Pavilion, which was built in the 1390s by the first of the Ashikaga shoguns, marked the beginning of the Muromachi period.

Muromachi period (1393–1568)
(Chinese Ming dynasty, 1368–1644)

The era of the devastating Onin wars and the refining influence of Zen on garden-making.

The mingling of the warrior classes with the imperial classes in Kyoto led to an extraordinary flowering of the arts. It saw the building of the Golden Pavilion in the 1390s and the Silver Pavilion in the 1470s, by Ashikaga shoguns, whose pond-filled stroll gardens were a departure from the earlier preference for boating lakes. The most important contribution of the Muromachi period was the creation of "dry water" gardens (*kare-sansui*) that used rocks set in gravel or sand to symbolize water. The most famous of these were the Daisen-in (c. 1513) and the Ryoan-ji (1499).

Momoyama period (1568–1603)
(Chinese Ming dynasty, 1368–1644)

The era of the unifiers and the rise of the tea masters and the merchant class.

Three successive military unifiers built gardens using larger rocks than before as an expression of power, but this excess was tempered by the modesty of an important new feature: the tea house and garden. The tea-ceremony ritual was popularized by a merchant called Rikyu, one of the most influential figures in Japan.

Right A garden of clipped shrubs, which are known as *o-karikomi*, at Sanzen-in, a garden from the Edo period.

Left The gardens around Nijo Castle, in Kyoto, were constructed at the beginning of the Edo period. These gardens used larger rocks than ever before and in greater numbers.

Edo period 1603–1867
(Chinese Qing dynasty, 1644–1911)

The era of National Isolation and the private stroll gardens.

In 1603, the Tokugawa shogunate moved to the eastern capital, Edo (now Tokyo), where strict social structures were enforced. The gardens of this period are mostly characterized by stroll gardens, the most famous of which is the Katsura Detached Palace, in Kyoto. With its numerous pond-side tea houses and buildings, as well as exquisite framed views, it possibly represents the last great peak in Japanese garden art.

Meanwhile, the city merchants and samurai developed the small courtyard garden, incorporating motifs from both the dry and tea gardens of earlier ages. In time, gardens in general would become more ostentatious, losing the depth and creative edge of their philosophical predecessors. Since 1867, however, when Japan re-opened to the West after over 200 years, gardens have explored the minimalist nature of Zen, the *avant-garde* and more naturalistic styles, although frequently incorporating traditional motifs such as the Mystic Isles.

Waves of Chinese influence

Before AD607, Japan was essentially a primitive culture that had received only a trickle of Chinese cultural influence through Korea. When the first Japanese ambassador to China arrived in Ji, the Chinese capital, in 607, he would have seen vast lake-and-island gardens, encircled by pavilions, surrounding the great imperial palaces.

In Chinese gardens, these islands were often used to represent the Mystic Isles, the mythical abode of the immortals. The Chinese emperor Han Wu had built his own lake and a fantastical island garden in the hope of enticing the immortals down to part with the secret elixir for eternal youth. The Mystic Isles were believed to float on the backs of turtles, while the immortals were carried around on the backs of cranes. Over the years, these myths had a huge impact on the Japanese imagination and, to this day, the Mystic Isles, cranes and turtles still feature prominently in Japanese gardens, usually in the form of carefully composed rock groupings. Rocks not only represented islands, however, but also came to symbolize Mount Shimusen, the central mountain in Buddhist mythology and an important mountain-water image that arrived in Japan.

Buddhism was a major force in Japan and it gained importance from the mid-6th century onwards, incorporating additional Chinese influences. However, even though the Emperor of Japan placed the country under the protection of the Buddha, Buddhism never usurped the status of the *kami*, which were the indigenous Shinto gods who were responsible for the emperor's existence and for the well-being of society.

Ponds were central to the Buddhist concept of paradise and became as central to Japanese gardens as they had been in China. The Amida Buddha's Land of Paradise Garden was described as being planted with gem-laden trees, while golden sands bordered lily-filled lakes. On these lakes, heavenly hosts waited for devout souls to give them a new birth in the realm of bliss on a lotus blossom. The great Amida garden of lakes and islands became the

Far left The Chinese myths of the Mystic Isles still inspire designers today. In the dry garden of Ryogen-in, created in the 1980s, stands the central mountainous island of Horai.

Left At Konchi-in lies a rock arrangement in the form of a crane. Cranes were said to carry the immortals on their backs.

Opposite A turtle island at Konchi-in where the head and flippers can be picked out from among rocks and clipped shrubs.

Left Ancient Chinese gardens displayed trees and fantastic rocks in their courtyards. The Japanese, although heavily influenced by the Chinese and often including rocks in a similar style, also had a preference for a more naturalistic approach to garden design.

dominant image of Nara- and Heian-style gardens. In AD 794, when the capital was moved to what is now Kyoto (Heian Kyo), the pond and winding-stream garden was the pre-eminent garden design. Gradually, during the Heian period, fuelled by the cultured society of Kyoto, a true Japanese garden style began to emerge, a style that slowly and indiscernibly blended Buddhism, the Mystic Isles and Shinto's sacred groves into the distinctive art form that is so recognizable today.

Geomancy

This is the Chinese science of divination, which affected the design of palaces, towns and gardens by its insistence that buildings, plants and rocks must be placed in a very precise manner, according to certain forces or lines of energy, to ensure that they were in balance and in tune with the natural order. If a placement was wrong, trouble and ill health could descend on the nation, a household or an individual. In fact, the choice of the site of the new city of Kyoto, modelled on the Chinese city of Chang'an and its palaces and gardens, followed Chinese geomantic principles. Each of the elements is linked to a direction: earth at the centre, water in the north, fire in the south, wood in the east and metal in the west. Other approaches to the elements also believed that each direction could represent colours, planets, seasons and guardian gods.

The principles of yin and yang are also part of geomancy, but are not always regarded as precise opposites. Most phenomena contain an element of both because bringing them together produces harmonious conditions. For example, combining water (yin) with the sun or fire (yang) creates the right conditions for making seeds germinate.

The next wave of influences on the Japanese garden also came from China, through her painters, the introduction of Zen Buddhism, and the tea-drinking ceremony.

Paintings

The Chinese artists of the Tang and Song dynasties painted mountains, pine trees beside waterfalls, streams falling into lakes, and paths weaving through rocks. These artists, more so than all of the great Chinese imperial parks, helped to influence the Japanese garden. Meanwhile, Japanese monks and artists who visited China saw temples of great beauty, as well as hermit monks and artists in huts and caves, and returned home with a desire to emulate the Chinese lifestyle and arts that they had encountered.

Zen

The Japanese monks – eager for a purer version of Buddhism without esoteric practices such as the worship of Buddha Amidha – found in China practitioners of Chan (or Zen, as it is known in Japan), a word derived from the Sanskrit *dyana*, which means meditation. Zen Buddhism places more focus on the individual and on his efforts to control his mind, especially through meditation, and the experience of "no-ness".

By the late 1500s, the Japanese Zen masters had become the next great garden-makers, once again inspired by Chinese and Japanese paintings featuring dry gardens of sand and rocks. Their gardens became increasingly abstract, often carrying hidden messages of Zen symbolism.

Above The gardens of Tenryu-ji, situated in Kyoto and created in the 1300s, were originally laid out by a Chinese gardener, but were changed at a later date to be more in sympathy with Japanese taste. For example, a Chinese-style wooden bridge was replaced by a series of natural rock slabs.

Right A Chinese-style full-moon bridge, which was a popular garden feature in Japan in the Edo period, spans an inlet to a pond in the Frank Cabot garden in Quebec, Canada. The semicircular curve of the bridge makes a complete circle with its reflection.

Tea gardens and ceremonies

The paintings, poetry and spirituality of the Chinese literati were not the only source of inspiration for the Japanese painters and Zen monks. The design of the Japanese tea house was also inspired by the rustic hermitages of the Chinese literati and the hermits residing in their mountain retreats. As a result, merchants and monks would develop a new style of garden, which included a path (known as a *roji*) that led to a tea house.

By the early 16th century, this evolved into the influential form of the tea garden, and Japanese garden design took a brand new, imaginative direction. The Japanese tea garden is one that is very familiar to Western eyes, containing key features such as lanterns, water basins and wells.

Modern and Western influences

Until 1852, when the Black Ships of the American navy fired their first few warning salvos at the Tokugawa shogunate to force the Japanese to open ports to trade with foreigners, the influence of the modern and Western world had been limited. Once these trading and communication channels opened, the influence of the West started to make its mark in technical and artistic terms. This was a two-way interaction, as the impact of Japanese culture in the West was also very significant.

The Japanese regime in 1852 was in a sad state of decline. However, shortly after the American attack, the long-suffering and impoverished imperial family replaced the shogunate that had held power for 250 years, and enjoyed a new ascendancy.

From the mid-19th century onwards Japan's influence on the West made itself felt, with Japanese prints and artefacts flooding Western markets, invigorating the art world and inspiring the Impressionists, among others. Great architects, such as Frank Lloyd Wright (1869–1959) and Charles Rennie Macintosh (1868–1928), found a raw simplicity in Japanese architecture and gardens. They also admired the beauty of natural materials, which they used in conjunction with their own modern materials – glass, concrete and steel.

In gardening terms, what has particularly appealed to Western eyes is the style of extraordinary gardens such as the Ryoan-ji, in Kyoto, whose brooding mystery affects people as much now as it did when it was built in the 1490s. This 15th-century, Zen-style garden influenced many Western designers who, although perhaps unfamiliar with the concepts of Zen, found an art form that gave expression to their own minimalist, atonal and *avant-garde* creations.

Opposite Mirei Shigemori, an artist and garden maker, redesigned the garden of Tofuku-ji in Kyoto, in the 1930s. He was the first to see the potential of the Japanese garden to become a vehicle for contemporary expression. He was also influenced by the Western art forms of the time.

Right This uneven chequerboard of stone squares sunk into a sea of moss and edged with curved roof tiles set on their edge is at the garden of Tofuku-ji, which harmonizes the natural, the architectural and the contemporary to become almost timeless.

While the West was absorbing Eastern influences, so the Japanese showed an extraordinary capacity to absorb other traditions, both digesting and reinventing them. There was (and still is), for example, a Japanese hunger for English-style gardens, which were initially copied, as Chinese gardens had been, before being absorbed into their own mainstream and given an Eastern slant.

By the 1930s, however, the design of more traditional Japanese gardens had become rather stale and clichéd, prompting one or two designers to re-evaluate the use of established materials and motifs. The greatest of these was Mirei Shigemori (1896–1975),

who made private and temple gardens from the 1930s to the 1950s. These were given a modern twist but, interestingly, still employed traditional motifs and natural materials as well as concrete.

Since the 1950s, more modern gardens have replaced natural boulders and rocks with raw, blasted, quarried materials, plastics and metals, much in the same way that the 17th-century garden blended the artificial with the natural. This blending of new materials, while retaining the pure simplicity of Zen gardens, is still the hallmark of contemporary Japanese design.

One of the latest movements in the evolution of the Japanese garden is towards a more natural style of garden design, featuring both native plantings and naturalistic streams. However, what also stands out with these contemporary Japanese gardens is that Japan cannot entirely shed its cultural and historical past and that, even now, the most up-to-date garden designs still hark back through the ages to the 11th-century Heian gardens in their use of natural materials, as was laid down in the 11th-century book of gardening, the *Sakuteiki*.

Left A Japanese tea garden, designed by Maureen Busby at the 2004 RHS Chelsea Flower Show in London. The main feature of a tea garden is a stepping-stone path that passes through a "wilderness". This contemporary version has a more cultivated feel, but uses many of the same ingredients as an authentic tea garden. A Japanese maple (*Acer palmatum*) shades a clump of Japanese iris (*Iris kaempferi*), both emerging from a mossy mound studded with ferns.

Opposite, top The roof garden of the Canadian Embassy in Tokyo, designed by the Buddhist monk Shunmyo Masuno in the 1990s, merges the dramatic forms inspired by the Rocky Mountains with traditional natural rocks and blasted quarried rocks, set among modern paving.

Opposite, bottom left A contemporary dry garden in the USA, designed by Terry Welch, uses exactly the same forms, materials and styles as the original dry gardens that were made in Japan in the 15th century. The original *kare-sansui* has bridged cultures and centuries to inspire countless artists worldwide.

Opposite, bottom right A dry garden in the Bloedel reserve on Bainbridge Island, Washington State, USA. Like many of the original *kare-sansui*, this well-executed design uses flat-topped rocks in a sea of sand, while the whole dry garden is contained within a frame of granite sets.

Design principles and inspirations

The Japanese garden possesses a style quite unlike any other in the world. This unique character can be attributed to a number of inspirational sources. For example, Japan is an archipelago of rugged coastlines and a volcanic mountainous landscape, with steep rocky streams that tumble through forests containing a wonderful variety of natural flora. The ancient Japanese believed that all of nature – the trees, rocks, mountains and water – possessed spirits and the power to draw the gods down to earth.

The rich mix of this wonderful natural topography and native flora, combined with imported Chinese culture, forms the basis of the Japanese garden. Nature has always been very carefully observed in these gardens, from the way a rock is placed to the outline of a pond or island, but they are also steeped in philosophy, geomancy, religion, myths, art and poetry.

Opposite The garden of Tenju-an, in Kyoto, is a superb example of the interplay between geometric, man-made and irregular, natural forms.

Above The dry garden at Jiko-in, Nara; a Japanese-style garden in England; the simplicity of the well-executed gardens of Koto-in.

Nature is not simply copied in the Japanese garden, but aspects of it are suggested or implied, from the careful pruning of pines to look old and wizened, to the use of sand as a substitute for water. Even in the most contemporary of gardens, it is possible to detect the images and pared-down outlines of natural landscapes, such as lakes, the sea, islands, waterfalls and streams.

The pervasive aesthetic in Japanese gardens is that of asymmetry, restraint, the unstated, and an inordinate attention to detail. This restraint is countered by a lively splash of colour in measured seasonal doses, unlike most Western gardens that often insist on year-round flower colour.

The relationship between homes and temples and their gardens also differs from many other cultures. Gardens are rarely used for play, but for contemplation. Views of gardens are often framed within a rectilinear framework of pillars and walls, and, where possible, draw in distant scenes. Buildings and garden structures are mostly constructed in timber, bamboo and reeds to create the perfect interface with nature. Paths are designed to weave around gardens, forcing the visitor into groves or to take in specially contrived views. These views are composed like paintings.

The careful use of space and the understated became highly developed by Zen monks who promoted the art of painting, calligraphy and gardening as a means of self-discipline and to arrive at an understanding of the mind and nature.

Above, from left The walkway at Sanzen-in provides a perfect viewing platform; a border combining roof tiles, charred post-tops, granite blocks and blue clay tiles; roof tiles against maples in autumn dress.

Opposite Marc Keane created this garden near Kyoto in a small, rectangular framework. Raked sand and a single maple in a mossy mound prove how little you need to create a perfect scene.

Shinto and the natural landscape

Although initially influenced by Chinese gardens, Japan's mountainous and coastal landscapes, coupled with a spiritual reverence for rocks and trees derived from their own native religion, Shinto, came to bear a powerful influence, making Japan's gardens into a unique art form.

Japan's topography

A mountainous archipelago of four main islands, Japan has hundreds of small rocky islets. The mountains, over 50 of them volcanic, are steep and wooded, scored with rocky streams, hot springs and rivers. In fact, most are still wooded up to their peaks because, until recently, Buddhism was the official religion and the eating of meat and fish was prohibited. This meant that, unlike other parts of the world, their hills and mountains have not been stripped by sheep, goats and cattle. To this day, natural features, such as mountains, rocks and streams, continue to inspire Japanese garden designers and are recurring features of the Japanese garden.

The Shintoists' influence

Japanese settlers arrived by sea, possibly from Korea, in the 3rd or 4th centuries AD. They farmed the coastal plains and developed wet-rice farming, a way of life that influenced their seasonal rites and social-value systems. Their indigenous religion was Shinto, which means "way of the gods". This was more or less displaced by, or merged with, Buddhism in the 6th century. Shinto involved animistic and pagan-style rituals, and centred round rocks, trees and plants. It was believed that these objects possessed spiritual aspects that could draw down the gods to earth. There were two kinds of gods or *kami*: those that descended from above and those that lived across the sea and gave birth to the main islands of Japan. These two sets of gods were symbolized by sacred rocks and sacred ponds. These rock and pond motifs occur again and again in Japanese gardens, both past and present.

The Shintoists believed that certain places in the wild were inhabited by the gods. To this day, you will still find trees wrapped in ropes near to shrines, as well as old trees and rocks that have become shrines in their own right. *Shime*, or the binding of objects

Opposite At the end of the Edo period, Japanese gardens had lost much of their original inspiration. Towards the end of the 19th century, the designer Ogawa (aka Ueji) made a welcome return to creating gardens where nature was his greatest teacher. This sympathy with nature recalled some of the first Japanese gardens of the 10th century, such as Syoko-ho-en, near Kyoto.

Right Before the advent of Buddhism, which arrived from China in the 6th century AD, the main religion of Japan was Shinto. Shintoists believed the gods could be lured to earth in sacred groves. Rocks and trees were bound in ropes to symbolize a sacred precinct. These spaces are believed to have had a profound influence on the Japanese garden.

The mountain motif

Another uniquely powerful influence over the imagination and gardens of the Chinese and the Japanese were mountains, which, through myth and religion, stand as the central feature of many of their garden designs. One of these myths (which developed off the Chinese coast) was of the Mystic Isles. There were five islands, one of which was called P'eng-lai, which later became Horai in Japan. These islands, like those of Japan, were large and mountainous, towering thousands of feet high, their sides steep and precipitous, reaching up to high plateaux rich in greenery. Here were misty blue valleys where all the beasts and birds were white, trees bore pearls, the flowers were fragrant and the fruits brought immortality to those who ate them. Along the shores of the islands lived blissfully happy Immortals in golden, silver and jade pleasure pavilions. The Immortals were not gods, but men who suffered no sickness or death, and developed supernatural powers, being able to float through the air. Sometimes they were carried on the backs of giant cranes, another key feature of the Japanese garden.

Originally the Mystic Isles floated about and were not fixed to the ocean floor. Then, the Supreme Ruler of the Universe commanded the islands to be secured by 15 enormous turtles, but, one day, a giant cast a net and caught six of them. Some others drifted away and were lost, leaving just three. The Japanese might well have believed that they already lived on these isles. Whatever the case, the island of Horai, the crane and the turtle became embedded in their gardens, even being reproduced in Mirei Shigemori's garden at the Tofukuji, created as recently as 1938.

Add to this ancient myth the divinities of Shinto, the natural landscape of Japan, the influence of the distantly revered and idealized landscapes of China, and the Lands of Paradise promised by some Buddhist sects, and the whole concoction becomes a fertile brew for the development of a very special and beautiful style of gardening.

or even people with rice straw ropes, may originally have been used to designate territory, while the bound artefacts symbolize land or islands. (Interestingly, the word *shima*, meaning "garden", comes from *shime*.)

Go-shintai ("the home of the gods") and *iwa-kura* ("boulder seats" or "seats of the gods") can also still be found throughout Japan. They have been purified and covered with layers of sand and gravel to become *shiki-no-himorogi*, or "sacred precincts". Some special rocks may even have been added.

Such rituals and sacred spaces had an important influence on the use of rocks in gardens and dry-landscape gardens. The interplay between the flat expanse of the sea (symbolized by sand or gravel) and the rugged immensity of rocks and old trees provided a kind of aesthetic that inspired the leap from the purely spiritual space of Shinto to the secular space of the garden. This aesthetic may also explain why the Chinese style of garden was not copied "religiously". Shinto and the natural landscape of Japan provided a fertile influence that adapted the Chinese style into something new.

Above In the dry garden at Ryogen-in, the three main symbols of the Mystic Isles are laid out in a sea of sand. In the foreground is a "turtle isle" (*kameshima*); back left is Mount Horai (Horai-san), the tallest of the Mystic Isles; with a "crane isle" (*tsurushima*) at the rear.

Right In the precincts of the Shinto shrine of Kamigano, Kyoto, sits this pair of sand cones. Pairs of cones in a sea of sand are also found in some Zen gardens, such as the famous Daisen-in, as symbols of purification and renewal.

Nature, the seasons and the *sakuteiki*

Looking out over an expanse of sand raked into perfect lines, set in a perfect rectangular courtyard with one or two rocks, and an azalea or two clipped so much that they barely flower, one might be forgiven for thinking that Japanese gardeners are more inclined to fly in the face of nature than sympathize with it. Yet Japan's own natural landscape of mountains, windswept pines, waterfalls and islands all directly inspires and informs their garden designs.

The natural world has been a constant feature of Japanese gardens from the early days of the Heian period (AD 785–1184), when ideas came straight from the landscape and the natural world, right up to more abstract and contemporary gardens that still demonstrate a profound understanding of nature. Indeed, whereas the Italian garden expresses an intellectual and philosophical vision of nature and the English garden is mainly based on the idealized world of the pastoral idyll, the Japanese do not always copy raw nature, but use it in a highly symbolic way. More specifically, in the 15th and 16th centuries, they turned increasingly to their great landscape painters for artistic inspiration, just as the late 18th-century English Picturesque garden was inspired by the paintings of Nicholas Poussin and Claude Lorraine. Together with nature, painting has been a common starting point for many gardening movements.

Poetry and plants

In the culture of the Heian period, as distinct from the later austere Zen and Muromachi periods, the aristocracy that had settled around the emperor, in Kyoto, enjoyed years of peaceful luxury. They wrote poetry, and became more and more detached from the day-to-day business of running the country. A kind of melancholic

Left The opening of the cherry blossom is celebrated up and down Japan as a symbol of spring. Samurai also saw the fleeting petals of the cherry blossom as symbolic of their own fragile mortality, revering it as a sign of loyalty to one's lord. Cherry trees have been planted in Japanese gardens since the Heian period.

Opposite Although many Westerners have the impression that Japanese gardens are dry and lifeless, nothing could be further from the truth. Japanese gardeners have a passion for plants, and their own natural flora is the envy of the world. By a streamside in Kyoto, clouds of *Spiraea* blossom are overhung by boughs of cherry blossom.

pessimism pervaded their lives. They believed that they were living in the Mappo, the Buddha's period of Ending Law, with declining social and religious mores. They hoped to be transported to his Western Paradise for an afterlife of eternal bliss by regularly chanting out the Buddha's name. This life was seen as a fleeting interlude, a dream between two realities. They depicted this Paradise as gardens filled with ponds that were dotted with islands.

So, the Heian aristocracy closely observed nature, noting every whim and expression as a sign and symbol to compare with love, death, honour and the great range of human emotions. These emotions were often symbolized by plants. In the two great novels of the time, *The Pillow Book* (AD995) by Sei Shonagon and the *Tale of Genji* (early 11th century) by Murasaki Shikibu, trees and flowers, as well as the weather, were used to describe human thoughts and desires.

The Japanese have always had a deep love of plants and use them profusely in their gardens. The early Heian gardens contained many flowering shrubs, such as kerria, deutzia, lespedeza, azalea and osmanthus, as well as cherries, maples, wild roses and irises.

Seasons

The seasons around Kyoto are fairly predictable, right down to the first rumblings of thunder over the mountains that herald the beginning of the rainy season in mid-summer. By then, the cherry blossom, wisteria and azalea will have long dropped their last blooms and the hydrangeas started to colour. At the same time, it will be sweltering in the sub-tropical south in Kyushu, while in northern Honshu and Hokkaido, trees growing below the melting snows on the mountain-sides will have yet to come into leaf. Apart from the northern reaches, most of Japan endures uncomfortably hot and rainy summers. This is why the cultured Heian elite in Kyoto placed such a strong emphasis on the two main garden seasons: spring (the most important) and autumn, an emphasis which still exists today. The seasons were also considered to be part of the geomantic system, with flowers being used to depict the cardinal lines of energy; good planting and design helped protect the household from misfortune.

In modern Japan, the plum and peach blossoms are the fanfare for spring, followed shortly by the cherry blossom. Then come the native camellias, azaleas and *floribunda* wisterias, while, in early summer, iris festivals are celebrated up and down Japan. The lotus, the enduring symbol of Buddhism, also flowers in summer. The autumn is marked by the Japanese maples (*Acer palmatum*) which grow in Japan's forests, as does *Enkianthus* which sets ablaze the hillsides and hillside temples at this time. Chrysanthemums, symbols of the imperial family, long life and good fortune, are grown especially for festivals in late autumn. In winter, the pine, cedar and bamboo are celebrated for their endurance.

The *Sakuteiki*

The earliest known treatise on gardening, the *Sakuteiki* – the subtitle of which was the "Setting of Stones" – was written in the mid-11th century, about 50 years after the *Tale of Genji*.

Left The plants that appear in autumn are as popular as the spring cherry blossom in Japan. The hillsides and temple gardens around Kyoto become ablaze with the fiery reds and yellows of *Acer palmatum*, as here in the garden of Tenju-an.

It was more of a technical journal for the select few, but many of its rules are still adhered to today, not for its superstitious element but due to its elemental precepts. Stones had "desires", and the book recommends several ways of listening to them, which was vital if they were (and still are) to be placed correctly in the Japanese garden, as if they are in the wild. The chapter headed "Nature" describes the remarkable and vivid use of the imagery of coastlines, streams, rocks, islands and waterfalls in garden design, and details a range of types with specific instructions. For example, stones can be used in different ways – perhaps placed in streams in order to modulate the flow of water, used as bottom or solitary stones, or as diffused stones to interrupt the flow of water. Furthermore, garden streams (*yarimizu*) can be created in various styles: as if they are flowing through a valley or as if they are broad rivers or mountain torrents. There are also descriptions of and instructions for creating different kinds of waterfall, all of which are relevant to the Japanese gardener today.

Above In the garden of Syoko-ho-en, Kyoto, the placement of the rocks and the pruning of the trees and shrubs follow the "desires" of nature. The hand of man is hidden well in this garden. In the foreground, the autumn-flowering toad-lily (*Tricyrtis*) is near the edge of a stream.

The garden streams often pour down a waterfall into a lake or pond. The lakes are dotted with islands and their shorelines punctuated by promontories. These were made of white sand to evoke the beaches of distant landscapes, while wind-swept ocean beaches, coves and undulating shorelines were planted with soft grasses. Islands also came in different guises, with rocky shores, for example, or in forest, meadow and wetland styles.

The earliest Japanese gardens, from the Heian period when the *Sakuteiki* was written, still have an important influence on modern garden designers who look to nature for inspiration. These gardens emphasize that we should observe but not slavishly copy nature, consulting the "genius of the place" before transforming it into art.

The influence of Zen

Zen was introduced to Japan from China by monks in the 13th century. Once established, it provided a consistent influence for all aspects of Japanese culture. The "no-ness" of the Zen philosophy, in particular, provided an important design philosophy for garden designers.

The original pioneer monks who introduced Zen to Japan initially met with a rather bleak response from the rather philistine military government based in Kamakura, south of present-day Kyoto. Two or three generations later, however, and Zen found new patrons among the rival warlords and the imperial family so that, by the early 1300s, there were some 300 Zen monasteries in Kamakura and Kyoto.

These temples, part of what was called the Five Mountain Network, promoted studies in a range of Chinese arts and philosophies. Apart from neo-Confucian metaphysics, the monks were also highly skilled in poetry, painting, calligraphy, architecture, ceramics and garden design. A less erudite group of rural monks, who were known as *Rinka* (meaning "forest"), practised in another network of Zen

temples and devoted themselves strictly to *Zazen*, or sitting Zen (meditation), as well as *koan* (the writing of riddles). Their self-discipline and loyalty to their masters appealed to the rising warrior class, the samurai, to whom the *Rinka* monks preached stern moralizing sermons. This philosophy was shared by the followers of Zen, whose teachers or masters also transmitted their values to their disciples. There were no written scriptures, though, and none of the trappings of esoteric Buddhism, such as mandalas, chanting and the reciting of scriptures, which had dominated Japanese life for the previous 500 years.

Zen and the dry garden

One particular monk called Dogan (1200–53), who lived during the Kamakura period, was well known for emphasizing the "no-ness" of all things (emptiness, void or non-substantiality). This aspect of Zen meant finding what might be called the "perfect expression of pure mind". Garden designers expressed this "no-ness" in the empty space of sand in dry gardens. Sand had already been used within Shinto sacred precincts, then in front of palaces for court ceremonies, before evolving into a representation of the sea or a white canvas for the painter-gardeners. Under the auspices of the Zen practitioners, the empty stretch of sand came to represent a meditative spiritual space. Sometimes, these dry gardens look like familiar landscapes, or imitated brush paintings, but, if they are stared at for long enough, especially by someone experienced at meditation, they can induce a sense of calm.

It was mostly the Zen monks who designed the extraordinary spaces known as *kare-sansui* (dry landscapes), which have since become synonymous with Japanese gardening, most notably at the famous dry gardens of Ryoan-ji and Daisen-in. Zen exercised (and carries on exercising) a strong influence over gardens, and it also gave greater precision and discipline to the already highly

Opposite The peerless garden of the Ryoan-ji has been studied intensely by artists, philosophers and Zen monks ever since it was first laid out in 1499. The composition of 15 rocks, set in a rectangle of sand, against a beautiful backdrop of an oil and clay wall overhung with trees, is a place of pilgrimage for hundreds of thousands of people.

Above Zen monks not only created gardens of simplicity, but were also drawn to the world of the Chinese scholar-hermit. Their response was to create tea houses and tea paths as places imbued with the spirit of Zen, in which to commune with each other in a secular world.

developed art of garden design. As a result there is no need to be steeped in the mysteries of Zen in order to appreciate the extraordinary beauty and sense of style or the pared-down, abstract visions of nature in these gardens.

Zen and the tea garden

The evolution of the tea garden had strong links to the Zen monks. Tea, used originally by monks as an aid to wakefulness during their long periods of meditation, soon became an important part of Buddhist rituals and ceremonies. So, it was only a short step for Zen monks, acting as both garden makers and tea-drinkers, to bring these two arts together.

Zen and today's gardens

When creating a Zen-style dry garden or even a tea garden, bear in mind the influences that created them. Many contemporary gardens are made up of a few rocks, a layer of sand or gravel, a bamboo plant or pine tree, and are glibly described as being very Japanese or, worse, very Zen. That can only be true, however, if there is no hint of the superfluous. Nor should any one feature dominate the design. Zen-style dry gardens and tea gardens should be imbued with a sense of purity and restraint. Only by understanding the importance

Opposite The Zen monk Shunmyo Masuno is a contemporary garden artist. Here, at the Canadian embassy in Tokyo, he has created a dry garden with natural rocks and sand, paying homage to the past and yet with the brave cutting edge of modernity.

Below In the same garden, natural rocks have been replaced by slabs of blasted quarry stone and assembled with fragments of the rock. The mountain image and empty space are features of the Zen garden.

of this can you attempt to create a Zen garden. Imitations may be in the style of a Japanese garden, but will not necessarily possess those qualities that a Zen garden-maker would seek. However, this does not mean that you cannot design dry-style gardens or tea gardens without a good knowledge of Zen, because the styles themselves have inherent aesthetic qualities that can be successfully copied.

So, while the first gardens of the 11th century were poetic readings of nature and the 15th-century gardens were inspired readings of the master landscape painters, the Zen gardens of both periods were disciplined attempts to understand the self and the universe. What this meant in practical terms was that there was an avoidance of the trite, the obvious and the emphatic. Unnecessary distractions and the use of excessive colour or form were avoided. The prime ingredients were the seven aspects of Zen aesthetics: asymmetry, simplicity, austere sublimity, naturalness, tranquility, subtle profundity and freedom from attachment. These qualities also applied to other art forms such as calligraphy and poetry.

Architecture and design

For every designer of gardens, the starting-point is invariably the house. This is especially true for Japanese garden designers. Up until the Edo period (1603–1867), all major garden styles evolved in towns and were defined by the layout of the main buildings, courtyards, entrances and boundaries.

The relationship between the garden and the architecture of the main house, temple and garden buildings is quite unlike that of the Western garden. In the West, the details and forms of the architecture seep out into the garden, especially in formal gardens, but the Japanese garden enjoys the interplay between the angularity of the architecture and that of natural forms.

Although dry and courtyard gardens are often contained within the rectilinear confines of garden walls, the forms of the gardens themselves are more like paintings held within a picture frame. In other styles of Japanese garden, the natural forms of stepping stones, rocks, pine boughs and bamboos are brought very close to the buildings. Although, in some cases, azaleas or camellias may be clipped into geometric forms to accentuate or even imitate the architecture, asymmetry and dynamic natural forms are preferred.

Shakkei

Many old houses and temples have verandahs with pillars which support the roofs. These pillars also frame a view of the garden. The views of the garden from indoors can be regarded, like those views over dry gardens, as if one was looking at a painting. The art of framing is even more important when a distant view can be captured – for example, the sight of Mount Fuji, near Tokyo, or Mount Hiei, near Kyoto. This technique is called *shakkei*, or borrowed scenery, but was once known by the more evocative term *ikedori*, meaning "captured alive". It was an important device that involved more than simply having a "nice view" from your house. *Shakkei* meant that prominent features could be drawn into the garden and become an intrinsic part of its overall composition.

Although most Westerners wishing to reproduce a Japanese-style garden will not own a Japanese-style home, they may have verandahs, sliding panels or garden buildings with the same type of interaction between the architecture and natural forms as the classic Japanese garden might possess.

Architectural overview

The Japanese buildings of the Nara and Heian periods, like their gardens, were more or less copies of the Chinese. By the Heian period the Japanese already showed a preference for the natural finish of timber than the more flamboyant painted building that would have been found in China at the time. Roofs were also less sweeping and curved than their Chinese counterparts.

Left The layout of the garden at Shoden-ji can be viewed from the verandah of the temple, drawing in the sacred mountain of Mount Hiei, a garden design technique known as *shakkei* or borrowed landscape.

The principal style of the Heian aristocratic homes was known as *shinden* (literally, "sleeping hall"). This main hall or *shinden* was set at the centre of a square building, with two adjacent wings to the sides for the concubines and wives. From these two wings, two corridors (the east and the west) led south to the main garden. In the space between these two corridors was an open, sand-covered courtyard which was reserved for ceremonies and entertainment. Through part of this courtyard, a stream might meander and feed into the main pond beyond.

At the end of the arms of corridors were pavilions, usually named after their primary function. The fishing pavilion was often built on stilts over the main pond, but was just as likely to have been used by musicians. Another pavilion may have covered the well or the spring that fed the pond.

Over the next 200 years, Japanese architecture evolved into smaller and more refined urban residences. By the Muromachi period, monks and samurai showed a marked preference for the *shoin* style. *Shoin* was a term that referred to the alcove which was set within one of the outer walls of the main building. This alcove had papered walls in order to allow light to illuminate a specially designed shelf or a desk for reading and writing. The *shoin* was a kind of library or study that, for the warriors and abbots,

symbolized their arrival as members of the intelligentsia or literati. This new architectural style was found in many temples and houses, which also had verandahs and sliding panels that opened up to view their gardens.

The tea house also employed some aspects of the *shoin* style, especially the alcove, but the general style of tea-house architecture was more rustic. The Japanese tea house, which was originally known as the "mountain place in the city", combined the rustic charm of the thatched hut (*soan*) with the sophistication of a more literary and urban style (*shoin*) of architecture. This hybrid style was, and still is, the most popular one for building tea houses and garden buildings.

The alcove of the tea house, which became known as the *tokonoma*, was a place in which to display works of art, especially calligraphy scrolls and poems, alongside simple country-style flower arrangements.

Right Sliding rice paper panel doors (*shoji*)
open up a view from a *tatami*-matted
tea-room at Isui-en, Nara. The square
opening and architectural lines interact with
the weaving stems of Japanese maples
(*Acer palmatum*), whose canopy of autumn
colouring provides a foreground to a view
over the stroll garden. Among mounds of
clipped azaleas, enkianthus and dwarf red
pine (*Pinus densiflora* 'Umbraculifera'),
a sandy path wanders around the edge of a
pond. Classic designs for the Edo period stroll
gardens include paths that wander around
ponds, visiting arbours, tea houses and
specially contrived views from particular
vantage points. Often famous "picture
postcard" landscapes were created to imitate
scenic spots from around Japan and China.

Understanding the designs

You do not really need to understand the essence of Japanese gardens in order to enjoy them, but if you want to design a successful Japanese garden, or see how they work, it does help to look beneath the surface and see what exactly is going on.

Despite the complexity of the different kinds of Japanese garden, ranging from pond and stream gardens to dry gardens, the common Western impression is of a small, carefully cultivated, highly stylized space, filled with clipped shrubs, rocks and stone artefacts, such as lanterns, pagodas and Buddhas. In reality, the finest Japanese gardens are larger than many Western city gardens, and the artefacts are quite superfluous to their design. What counts is the spirit of the garden, and how the different elements are balanced.

The spirit of nature

The beauty of many Japanese gardens lies in their sublime vision of nature. The pleasure in the poetic beauty of flowers and cherry blossom that was so evident in the 11th century, although no longer paramount, lingers on. It is also important to remember, when trying to create a Japanese garden, how the Japanese revered their gods and the landscape gods. You need to have an instinctive feeling for, say, an open ocean, the way a river flows, and how a mountain range is encircled by mist to successfully create your garden. In other words, you need to appreciate the spirit of *yugen* ("hidden depth"), where something grand elevates the soul. In order to tap into this spirit, you need to have a highly tuned feeling for nature. So, for example, when creating a pond, make sure that it echoes the outline of a natural lake. This will also help to dictate the design or layout of any waterfalls, banks, rock scatterings or plants at the water's edge.

Although water and rocks are the foundation of the garden, the design of any artefacts and buildings follows a carefully observed and orchestrated relationship between the natural and man-made. So, the finely polished wooden panels of the tea house might be in-filled with rough plaster, while the wooden support posts might still have their bark on. The concept of *wabi-sabi* is equally important. This was a poetic term adopted by the tea masters in order to describe a quality of raw simple beauty, touched with the patina of age.

The value of asymmetry

Symmetry is rarely found in Japanese gardens. Occasionally an entranceway will have straight paths bordered by a pair of hedges or a view might be framed by rugged pine trees, but symmetry is

Left The roofline of the Great Buddha Temple of Nara is highlighted by the late-evening sun. The view of the temple and the hills is "borrowed" by the garden of Isui-en to become part of the garden picture.

generally seen as something which hems in the imagination. In the absence of symmetry, you need to create a design that has a balanced composition, as well as a good sense of proportion between open and enclosed areas, and an easy transition from one section of the garden to another. This approach will ensure that nothing jars the eye, while there is enough empty space (or void) in which the imagination can roam. The need for free-flowing movement does not only apply to the transition from area to area, but also to specific ingredients. So, paths and streams must meander and wander as they do in the wild, and ponds must have natural outlines.

Creating layers of interest

Looking at old Japanese paintings, we can understand the use of different layers of interest for creating a balanced composition, as well as the play of light and shade. In the past, Japanese garden designers copied the approach of painters, searching for the essence of a landscape, framing it and then dividing it into a balanced mix of foreground, middle and distance. We can adopt the same approach in today's Japanese garden. The foreground might be sand or grass, featuring a water basin, rock or plant.

Right The tea path is often divided into two halves, with a gate marking the approach to the garden around the tea house. Here, the path is highly stylized and uses a mixture of random and square-edged paving.

Left Japanese gardeners have always drawn their inspiration from paintings as well as nature. Monchromatic ink paintings in particular, with their simple brushwork, were imitated by the makers of Zen dry gardens.

The middle section might incorporate a pond or an implied one, using sand, island groups of rocks, and a weathered pine tree or clipped shrub. In the background there might be more open space and just the occasional rock. Additional features could include a grotto by the edge of the pond, bridges crossing inlets or streams entering the pool from waterfalls. Any higher ground beyond the pond might be backed by hedges, a bamboo screen or, if you have sufficient space, an artificial hill. The latter can often be created with the piled-up excavated soil from making a pond. The shape and size of these hills might suggest a distant range, or even the sacred Mount Lu, a Buddhist pilgrimage site in China. Planting the top and sides of the hills with dwarf or clipped pines can help to give an illusion of distance.

Japanese garden styles

The various styles of Japanese garden have evolved for over a millennium. During that time, there have been dramatic leaps of cultural and historic change that have clearly helped to create a few very distinctive styles. It is limiting to try to break down these styles into different types because there is so much overlap between them. The five styles described here, however, do make it simpler to understand the way a Japanese garden might be developed.

Many of us may not have the room to recreate the pond, stream and island gardens of the Heian period, but we can still emulate their simplicity of design and reverence for nature. In these gardens, there were no lanterns, tea houses or dry gardens, which would feature in the later stroll gardens. They were simply about pleasure and the perpetuation of the myths of immortality. They were also a place for celebrating flowers and the changing seasons.

Opposite A stream enters a pool at Murin-an, in Kyoto, a late-19th century stroll garden. The pond edge has a shingle-beach border.

Above, from left Guests at the entrance to a tea-room, Nanzen-ji; a *tsukubai* at Nijo castle; the entrance gate to a tea garden at Nijo castle.

One of the familiar types of Japanese garden is the dry or Zen garden, featuring small, often enclosed, expanses of sand with one or two rocks set in the sand. Although inspired by Zen and brush–and–ink paintings, these gardens have a contemporary appeal for those gardeners seeking simplicity and minimalism. The dry garden suits all kinds of spaces where a more conventional garden might be impossible or impracticable.

The tea garden also has as much relevance today as it did in the 16th century, but it is more difficult to copy. However, with a little knowledge of the philosophy behind the tea ceremony, it would be possible to reproduce one.

The most familiar style, after the dry garden, is the stroll garden. This is an amalgam of all of the preceding styles but is most suitable for those with a larger garden. Most stroll gardens include a small central pond with a circulating path that weaves through groves of cherries, crosses over bridges, and visits tea houses and arbours, often with views over the pond.

The courtyard garden, like the stroll garden, includes many motifs from other garden styles. Usually the smallest of the Japanese gardens, courtyard gardens are often simple in design and easier to reproduce. All that is needed to create one is a rock or two, a lantern, and a bamboo or pine tree; simplicity and restraint will give the most satisfying results.

Above, from left Purification is ritualized by the Japanese; a carp stone at the base of a waterfall symbolizes an individual's strivings; the Mystic Isle rock arrangement at Tofuku-ji has immense power and drama.

Opposite At the Heian shrine, in Kyoto, the staggered stepping stones are made of recycled bridge piers and temple column bases. Borrowing old architectural fragments is known as *mitate* ("to see anew").

Pond and stream gardens

Ponds, lakes and streams have always been central to the Japanese garden, instilling a sense of tranquillity, joy and calm. You do not need a particularly large garden to include an expanse of water, although the results will obviously be much more dramatic if you are able to construct a feature of some size and presence.

We can gain some inspiration for the design of present-day pond and stream gardens by looking briefly at a famous example from Japan's past, Motsu-ji, which is one of the very few surviving pond and island gardens from the 12th century. Today, you can still see Motsu-ji's great lake, which is bordered by formal iris beds and dramatic rock arrangements. Nothing remains of the palatial and temple complexes, but remarkably there are sufficient vestiges of this garden to conjure up images of how it might have been used. These glimpses into the past are intriguing. Guests would sit by streams which wove through meadows before entering the lake at great "winding-water" banquets. Resplendent garden parties were held, in which painted dragon barges, filled with musicians who

were dressed in elaborate costumes, were oared and punted around the lakes. At special ceremonies, they might pray for rain for the rice fields or evoke Amida Buddha in his Paradise garden.

The lakes were broad and sunny, glimmering under the sun, moon and stars, while weeping willows swayed and shaded their banks. Birds and fish would have added colour and movement to this intoxicating scene. The lakes had a pebbled bottom or were edged with beaches of silver sand and backed by low hills planted with trees and shrubs. This style of pond garden differs from the later stroll gardens by having none of the more familiar tea houses, lanterns or water basins. Instead, these were ponds with islands, often linked by bridges.

Pond gardens remained popular in Japan, but, as they became smaller, their outline became increasingly complex and indented and the rock arrangements more artistic and painterly. The sumptuous gowns of the ladies of the Heian period would have made it impossible for them to stroll around the lakeside gardens, but the later ponds of the Kamakura and Muromachi periods, which were too small for boating parties in barges, formed part of the first real stroll gardens, a style of Japanese garden that we will

Left A path circles a naturalistic pond in the garden of the Golden Pavilion (Kinkakuji). This 14th-century garden was modelled on early pond gardens. The lake is studded with pine-clad islands.

Opposite The gardens of the Heian shrine, in Kyoto, were created in the late 19th century to recreate the spirit of the 10th- and 11th-century gardens of the Heian period. The main feature of these gardens was a large boating lake. Here, an island planted with pines and a weeping cherry is linked to the mainland with large, granite slab bridges.

look at later on. Most of these pond and stream gardens were confined within walls, which meant that their size was fairly limited, a factor that makes it easier for us to imagine how they can be created in smaller Western gardens.

In trying to reproduce such a style, one has to imagine a far more poetic time, as well as one in which there was a far greater reverence for nature. While later gardens were influenced more by painters and Zen philosophy, the Heian pond garden takes nature in its well-observed form as its main guide.

The *Sakuteiki*, written in Heian times, names many forms of pond styles, islands, streams and waterfalls, and even notes how best to plant trees. We can draw on this ancient work for inspiration when designing pond and stream gardens. For example, when placing rocks or choosing the course of a stream, you need follow the "desire" or "request" of the stone or water. Inanimate rocks were, and still are, thought to possess personalities that must be treated with respect. By doing this, you would achieve a balanced, harmonious design.

It is also important to remember that the design of a water garden should be asymmetrical, even though the adjoining architecture may be symmetrical. The interplay between the formal architecture and the informality of the garden is part of the genius of Japanese gardens. The design of the pond is key, and achieving a pleasing shape is vital to the success of the finished pond.

Turtle and crane motifs

Another main feature of the pond and stream garden was the group of islands that represented the Isles of the Immortals. Some of these took the form of turtles and cranes. They can be included in today's garden, although it is important to point out that Japanese representations of the crane or turtle are rarely naturalistic. The crane island is made up of a group of rocks, with one taller rock usually sitting up like a wing. In the groups of rocks representing the turtles, the head and flippers are sometimes discernible, but more often the image is utterly abstract and only a trained eye can appreciate what is being depicted.

The turtle and crane motifs are not essential to a pond and stream garden, but they can be included in today's pond garden if they are treated with some sensitivity. To recreate a crane or turtle island, look at some famous examples. You will find that some are made entirely of groups of rocks, while others are islands of earth

Opposite The original garden of the Moss temple was a 12th-century pond and stream garden, with islands linked by wooden bridges. The serenity and tranquillity of this garden is enhanced by the soft green of mosses and the scattered leaves of maples in autumn.

with rocks protruding into the lake, which can be discerned as flippers, a tail or a head. Whatever you do, do not attempt to create literal reproductions of these animals.

Designing a pond and stream garden

The pond or lake is the central feature of this style of garden and should be large enough and deep enough for a small boat, which can be kept moored to a stone or kept visible in an open-sided, ornate, Chinese-style boathouse. There should be at least one island in the pond. There were often two islands, both being linked by bridges. By the 14th century, when the ponds became smaller, the curved Chinese bridges were replaced by bridges made from less ornate materials such as rocks or unpainted timber. Small isolated islands can be planted with pine trees or grasses.

The outline of the pond can be indented with coves, beaches and grottoes. The land around the pond might be hilly, with the hills planted naturalistically with groups of trees. You can easily create a pond garden planted with iris beds and dotted with well-placed rock arrangements, possibly with a gently sloping, sandy beach area. Imagine recreating those resplendent outdoor celebrations with an *al-fresco* pondside supper for friends, perhaps lit with some paper lanterns.

There is a general nostalgia in Japan for this romantic period in Japan's history, exemplified by the stories in the *Tales of Genji* by Murasaki Shikibu. Although written in the 11th century, this is still a very popular novel. In it you will find numerous references to many kinds of plants and to boating parties. In the 17th century, at the Katsura Palace, and in the 19th century, after the restoration of the emperor as the head of state, some gardens were created to reawaken the spirit of those times. So, although this style of garden is very old, it still has a place in the hearts of the Japanese today. The naturalistic aesthetic makes it all the more relevant in times when nature is so much under threat, especially in Japan.

Top Pine islands, similar to those found off the coast of Japan, have been reproduced in the pond surrounding the Golden Pavilion. The beautifully pruned pines are reflected in the water.

Above Another pine island in the tranquil lake setting of the Heian shrine, in Kyoto.

Right The pond in the garden of Tenju–an. Ponds were originally used for boating parties for poetry readings, chanting and music. As ponds became smaller, as here, strolling took over from boating. The atmosphere of the Heian period was captured in *The Tales of Genji*, a novel of the 11th century, and throughout the history of Japanese gardens, designers have tried to recreate its romantic evocations. The fleeting colour of maple leaves in autumn was a special poetic subject of those times. Tenju–an, part of the Nanze–ji complex, in Kyoto, was originally built as a villa for a retired emperor in 1267, but this was destroyed by fire, and the present temple was built in 1602. Much of the garden dates back to the 13th century, with its simple design of two ponds, two islands and rock arrangements around a waterfall.

Garden plan | A pond garden

The design of this pond garden would suit those with a large garden. The main feature is the pond fed by a winding stream or by a spring spilling over a waterfall. Pine islands and rocky islets are artfully placed, some of them reached by Chinese-style bridges and viewed from a pavilion that might double as a boat house. The overall feel of the planting and rock placement is naturalistic.

How to construct a pine island

A pond garden is suitable in combination with a small pine island. Although it is possible to build an island after the pond has been built, it is always advisable to consider the addition of an island during the pool-building process, rather than as an afterthought because the pool will need emptying to build on the lining. The diagram below explains how to install a dry island before the pond is constructed.

1 If it is considered at the design stage, an island can be "dry". Create a large mound of soil in the centre of the pool during the initial excavation.

2 Lay the underlay and flexible liner over the top of the soil mound. Cut a hole in the underlay and liner so that an area of soil is exposed. Ensure that the liner is taken well above the waterline.

3 Add a further mound of soil on top of the foundation to create a gently curving island. Stack rocks on top of each other all around the edge of the island to hold the dry soil in place.

4 Because the liner is taken above the waterline, the mound of soil is kept dry.

Gravel path

Rocky stream

Small bridge over winding stream

Building a pine island

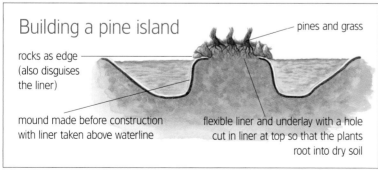

pines and grass

rocks as edge (also disguises the liner)

mound made before construction with liner taken above waterline

flexible liner and underlay with a hole cut in liner at top so that the plants root into dry soil

Plant list

1 Black pine
(*Pinus thunbergii*)

2 Cherry (*Prunus serrulata*
varieites)

3 Japanese maples
(*Acer palmatum*)

Maple grove

③

Small hill with waterfall

Rock groupings

Red Chinese bridge

Pine island with rocky shoreline

Rocky shoreline

Turtle island supporting
mountain horai

Rowing boat

Wooden boathouse

Above Windswept pine islands are
often modelled on those found off
the coast of Japan.

Above The arrangement of rocky
islets is often taken from the
myths of the Mystic Isles. This one
is symbolic of Mount Horai.

Above Winding streams emulate
a natural type of stream, with the
rocks used to modulate the flow.

Above Heian garden buildings
and bridges were often copies of
those found in China at the time.

Dry gardens

Often referred to as *kare-sansui*, which literally means "dry-mountain water", dry gardens are a style of garden in which water has been replaced by sand, gravel or pebbles. They have also become synonymous with what we now often regard as a Zen garden.

Dry gardens have inspired garden designers throughout the world to try to emulate and reproduce their style. An understanding or, better still, an experience of Zen will help you to find their spiritual essence, but another way to look at dry gardens is to see them as minimalist landscapes. Looking at Japanese brush paintings, by Sesshu, for example, can be a source of inspiration.

Origins of the dry garden

Before looking at the main features of the "dry garden" and at how it can be successfully created in the West, it will be helpful to look at some of the historical, artistic and religious principles behind this unique garden style. The precise origins of such "dry gardens" remain a little obscure. References to dry landscapes occur as early as the 11th century, but they refer to the natural placement of rocks in grass or moss, and not to water. It is possible that the early Shinto shrines were a starting point. The great Shinto shrines at Ise stand in vast rectangles of gravel. This gravel was replaced every 20 years as part of the rituals of renewal and cleansing, while rocks were (and still are) used to represent the Buddha and the Buddhist Trinity. The earliest dry-rock arrangements that preceded the *kare-sansui* may have been at Joeji-in, near Yamaguchi, where a collection of rocks was laid in an area of moss between the temple and the pond. This garden, created in the mid-1400s, is attributed to Sesshu, the great Japanese painter who reproduced his angular brush strokes in the garden using flat-topped and angular rocks. Sesshu possessed a rare combination of talents, being a painter, monk and gardener.

These gardens were not created because of a natural absence of water. Indeed, there is an abundance of water in many of the temple gardens around Kyoto. At the Ryoan-ji, for example, there is a large pond on the other side of the wall from the dry garden.

Left Dry-rock arrangements are often centred around a main stone with smaller stones around it. The main stone may have symbolized the Buddha, the sacred mountain of Shimusen, or Mount Horai of the Mystic Isles. This arrangement stands on an island of moss, overhung by maples and a clipped holly.

Opposite The raked circles of sand represent the eight rough seas; the hills of moss, the five sacred mountains; and the rocks represent islands – all tell the story of the myths of the Isles of the Immortals.

There were two main reasons for the creation of dry gardens. One was based on the principles of Japanese painters whose work inspired a monochromatic treatment of the landscape, and the second was linked to the philosophy of Zen. Most dry gardens appear in Zen temples and are associated with Zen Buddhism and meditation.

The dry gardens in Zen temples tend to be framed within rectangular courtyards close to the abbot's quarters (*hojo*). They can be viewed as paintings, illustrating distant and idealized landscapes "hung" within their rectangular frame. As garden style evolved throughout the 15th century, its influences shifted away from paintings that inspired natural landscapes towards paintings as a means of teaching the tenets of Zen.

In Zen, the disciple reaches his true self by diverting his gaze from the material to the spiritual world. Through meditation, he can experience what is known as the "void", a formless state of no-self, which Zen defines as the original face of man. Time spent in this state is a form of spiritual renewal. This "meditative void" can be equated to those areas of unpainted whiteness on a canvas and to the empty space of raked sand in a dry garden. Whereas lay people might look at a Zen garden and see islands in an ocean or mountain tops circled in mist, Zen practitioners will simply see space, a reflection of the infinite space that lies deep within us. Many of the arts of Zen employ the use of space to encourage this kind of self-awareness.

Ryoan-ji

The Ryoan-ji, in Kyoto, is a timeless example of the exceptional degree of artistry and deep understanding that painters, monks and garden-makers had in the late 15th century, when it is thought that this garden was constructed. The Ryoan-ji is a rectangular courtyard bordered on three sides by a clay and oil wall and on

Below Some of the first *kare-sansui*, or dry gardens, were created by Sesshu in the late 15th century. At Joeji-in, he took the unusual step of setting the rocks in the mossy grass between the temple and the pond.

the other by the abbot's quarters where a long verandah overlooks the garden from about 75cm (2$\frac{1}{2}$ft) above the level of the garden. The area is about the size of a tennis court, and is neatly edged in a frame of blue-grey tiles. The whole of the inner space is spread with a fine, silvery grey quartzite grit that is raked daily along its length in parallel lines. This "sea" of sand is the background canvas to 15 rocks in five groups (of 5-2-3-2-3), fringed by moss. This pattern recurs throughout the Far East, even in the rhythm of music and the chanting of Buddhist texts. The parallel lines of raked gravel break their pattern and form circles around the groups like waves lapping against island shores.

The magical way that the rocks are grouped and spaced has gripped generations of visitors, and not just monks, artists, poets and gardeners. No one knows the exact meaning of these groupings. Some have described them as possibly a tiger taking her cubs across a river, while others see them as mountains in the mist or as islands surrounded by sea. One reason for this puzzle is that Zen practitioners probably started with an idea, but ended up focusing on universal truths and abstract, natural shapes. When creating your own arrangements, bear in mind that the setting of the stones should "follow their own desire". The stones or rocks need not be particularly exceptional in themselves and should not be set as a piece of sculpture.

Designing a dry garden

To create a dry garden, first imagine a distant misty mountain landscape, a stream with waterfalls or a rocky shoreline. Look at how streams and rivers flow, how waves lap against rocks, and you will learn how to use the inspiration of nature to make raked patterns around rocks. Once you have composed a picture in your mind, then let go of the superfluous, allow the essence of the composition to take over, and minimize it. Remember that unfilled space is as important as space containing objects or plants. This "minimalism" has inspired many contemporary garden designers to reproduce the

dry garden in modern urban environments. After all, dry gardens were often created in domestic courtyards, not just in Zen temples. A simple composition could be created with a rock or two, a stone lantern, a water basin and section of bamboo fence in a stretch of sand.

Dry gardens do not only use sand and rocks, but also plants. At the garden of the Shoden-ji, in north-west Kyoto, rocks have been replaced by mounds of clipped azaleas in more or less the same kind of pattern as at the Ryoan-ji. The azaleas are clipped so much that they do not flower very well, but form is considered far more important than colour in this style of Japanese garden. If you liken these gardens to the monochrome paintings that inspired them, it is clear why colour is of little or no importance, while composition and space are paramount.

Dry gardens may appear to be quintessentially Japanese, but the appeal of their pared-down, minimalist style is both universal and contemporary. Once you have understood how the original 15th-century dry gardens were created, you may want to employ new, exciting methods of expressing the same principles, but in ways and with materials that are more relevant to your own culture, landscape and the materials that are readily available to you.

Left At Nanzen-ji, in Kyoto, built in 1264, over two-thirds of the dry garden is comprised of sand. The remainder is dedicated to this group of rocks and shrubs. The rocks are large and impressive, and are composed to display the innate quality of the stones. This feature is more characteristic of 17th-century dry gardens than of the carefully assembled groupings of the original dry gardens of the 15th century. The large stone to the left is balanced by the camellia and rock to the right and linked by the flat stone and clipped azaleas that lie between them. The result is a relaxed and elegant picture, completed by a well-layered red pine, the rounded camellia and the surrounding temple architecture and hills.

Garden plan | A dry garden

The best place for a dry garden is an enclosed courtyard bounded by walls or fences. This frames the garden so it can be seen as a painting "hung" within its frame. Dry gardens use sand to imitate ponds, streams and the sea, while rocks may be arranged like a waterfall. The deeper Zen meaning of these dry gardens is one of emptiness of mind, a goal of Zen meditation, invariably interpreted through an empty area of sand. Although many dry gardens have no plants in them, there may be an artfully placed wizened pine, clipped azalea or mound of moss. The whole garden should possess an air of restraint.

How to set rocks in gravel

1 Select your rock, ensuring that you have the means to handle it and get it into your garden. The easiest way to lift large rocks is with a mini-digger, or a small tractor with lift mechanisms.
2 Wire ropes and chains can be used to strap the rock, but the use of tough nylon/canvas fibre straps will minimize damage to the rock's surface. Wire ropes are easier to remove if they become trapped beneath a rock, whereas you may need to dig out straps. In Japan, tripods and pulleys lift and move rocks over small distances.
3 Decide which part of the rock will be visible and which part will be buried. This depends on the rock; a tall, upright rock will need to be buried deeper than a wide, flat one. Show off as much of the rock as possible, but make it appear to be buried deeply.
4 Dig the hole slightly deeper than you need to so that you can place smaller support wedging stones under and around the main rock to support it and to help obtain the best angle.
5 If you can, try the rock in different positions and angles before removing the straps, standing back to see if it "feels" natural.
6 Fill in tightly with soil around the main rock and its support stones. Soil with some clay content will be firmer than one that is loose and sandy.
7 Once in place, check the rock for stability.

Above Plum trees *(Prunus mume)* can live a long time.

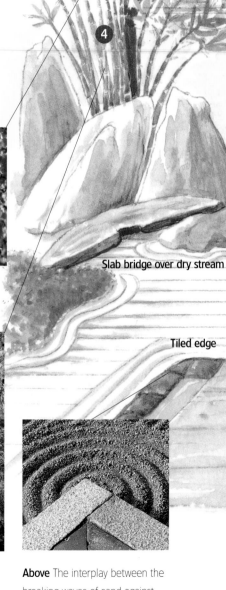

Slab bridge over dry stream

Tiled edge

Above Black bamboo is suitable to include as it does not get too big or spread around.

Above The interplay between the breaking waves of sand against the tiled "frame" of the garden.

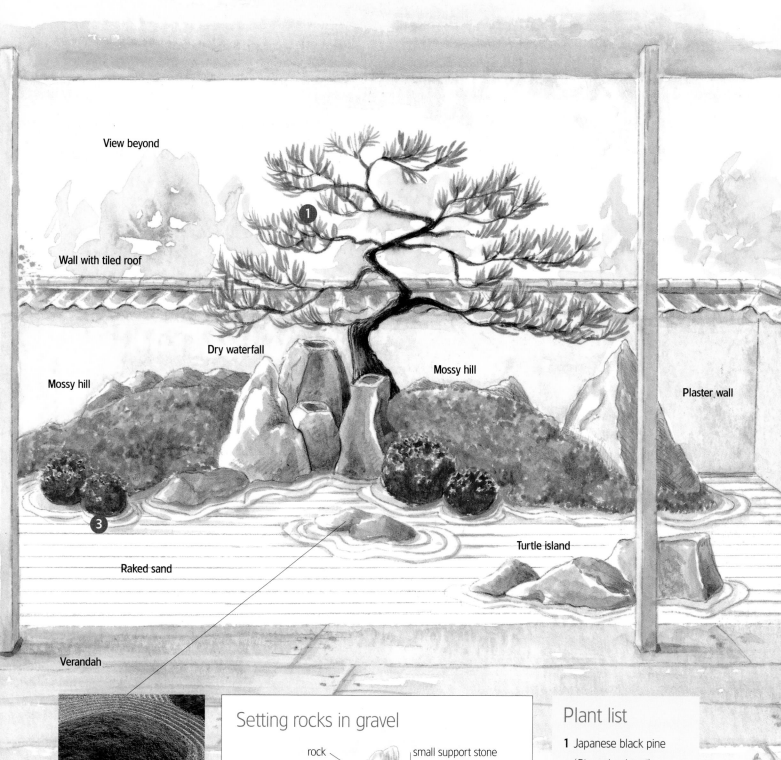

View beyond

Wall with tiled roof

Dry waterfall

Mossy hill

Mossy hill

Plaster wall

Raked sand

Turtle island

Verandah

Above Mossy mounds may need frequent watering to keep them fresh and green.

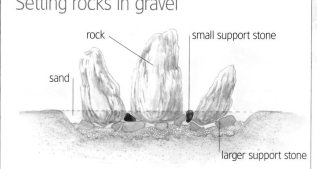

Setting rocks in gravel

rock

small support stone

sand

larger support stone

Plant list

1 Japanese black pine (*Pinus thunbergii*)

2 Spring plum (*Prunus* species)

3 Clipped azalea

4 Black bamboo (*Phyllostachys nigra*)

Tea gardens

Easily adapted for the modern garden, the design and philosophy of the tea garden suits contemporary city life as much as it did in the 16th century. Each element of a tea garden – for example, the stepping stones, lanterns, water basins and even the tea house itself – can easily be created using modern materials.

Once the significance of the tea garden has been grasped, you can be as creative as you want, as the great tea masters were 300 years ago. While one tea master might have preferred a natural look, another might have liked a creative mix of the man-made and the natural. Such adaptability is the main reason why tea houses and gardens have never died out, reappearing in stroll gardens and courtyard gardens from the 17th century to the present.

The introduction of tea

Tea, imported from China, had been drunk at the imperial court since the 9th century, but its cultivation did not start in Japan until the 13th century. The Buddhist monk Eisai, returning from his pilgrimages to China, is attributed with introducing both the precepts of Zen Buddhism and a collection of tea plants to Japan.

Tea was drunk by Buddhist monks as an aid to wakefulness during their long hours of meditation and also became popular among a class of intellectuals, poets, samurai and merchants towards the end of the 15th century. The monks and intellectuals brought the worlds of Zen Buddhism, poetry, pottery and art appreciation into the theatre of tea-drinking to create what is

known as the "tea ceremony", drawing the simple act of drinking tea into the realm of high art. By the mid-16th century, tea ceremonies, tea houses and tea gardens were part of the culture of Japan.

Tea houses

Ceremonies for drinking tea were mostly held in tea houses. The first great tea masters of the 16th century built their tea houses to imitate the mountain-side hermitages of the Chinese sages. These sages were learned in the arts, philosophies and religions of their

Opposite The most important feature of the tea garden is the path that leads to the tea house. Along this path, the guest may encounter a gateway, sometimes known as a stooping gate, which opens into the environs of the tea house itself.

Right The style of the roji, or tea path, evolved over the centuries, from one that was natural and simple to a more artful and complex style, like this one at Nanzen-ji. This path is made up of a mixture of cobbles, rectangular and round paving, and a temple pillar base.

time. The Japanese built their own style of hermitage that evolved into the tea house, not in the mountains, but right in their back gardens in cities like Kyoto, Nara and the port of Sakai, near present-day Osaka. The gardens around these "mountain places in the city", as they became known, were originally paths, symbolizing those taken by pilgrims on their way to meet the sages in their hermitages. The tea garden, or *roji*, which means "dewy path" or "dewy ground", evokes those mountain paths and evolved to include an elaborate set of sophisticated symbols.

Tea gardens generally open with a main gate, where guests enter the first half of the garden, known as the outer *roji*. The guests might then be asked to wait before being led by their host deeper into the garden, then to the tea house itself. On the way, they might pass through a middle "stooping gate", perhaps with a lantern nearby, designed to force the guest to bow slightly. This was a moment of enforced humility to stimulate an awareness of the "material" world he was leaving behind and of the higher and purer realms of consciousness that he would encounter in the tea house.

After passing under the stooping gate the guest would enter the inner *roji* that surrounded the tea house. This part of the garden was the "wilderness" which approximated the wild mountain landscape that might surround a Chinese hermitage. The guests would then wash their hands and mouths at a low basin called the *tsukubai* (or "stooping basin"). The *tsukubai* is a lower style of basin than the *chozubachi*, the taller water basins more frequently found near the verandahs of the main house. A lantern often accompanies the *tsukubai*, as many tea ceremonies took place in the evening.

After cleansing himself, the guest would proceed to the tea house, remove his shoes and enter through a small hatch-like

Top left A waiting booth at Chikurin-in, a tea garden a few miles from Kyoto. This type of shelter is sited near the beginning of a tea path, as a place for guests to gather until invited to proceed to the tea house.

Left A *tsukubai*, or water basin, is placed for guests to cleanse themselves before entering the tea house. A *tsukubai* is usually accompanied, like this one, by a lantern.

Opposite A bamboo panel tied with jute is framed between two branches. At the step, guests remove their shoes before entering the tea house.

entrance, the *nigiriguchi*. This small entrance was deliberately made too small for a samurai to enter with his sword still attached, so some tea houses had special racks built to hold swords.

Construction and materials

The tea house was often built as a rustic thatched hut but constructed with the finest planed timber. Elegant rush matting, called *tatamis*, lined the floor. Once inside, the guest would admire a seasonal flower arrangement and a pertinent calligraphy hanging in an alcove. The tea ceremony would then begin. The rusticity of the tea house combined with the refinement of domestic and temple architecture to create a whole new language in garden architecture, a craft that is still studied today.

Below The interior of a tea house at Toji-in. The materials are natural and simple, but the craftsmanship is detailed and refined. Tea houses are often secluded in groves, but here panels create views of the garden.

Major figures

The greatest tea master was the 16th-century Sen no Rikyu, who had a preference for the rustic and the rough. His successors, like Furuta Oribe and Kobori Enshu, who created gardens in the early 17th century, were from the samurai class and had more of a taste for man-made materials. By the 17th century, tea paths might include more formal square paving and millstones. The tea houses also changed, becoming more refined, more open and less humble. Later still, tea houses evolved into tea arbours, where tea might be drunk while overlooking the garden. The changing aesthetic from the Muromachi period through to the Edo period shows a slow evolution from *wabi-sabi* ("withered loneliness"), indicating a taste for the impoverished, to a more playful and artistic one (*asobi*).

Below Inside the tea house or tea room is a specially designed alcove (*tokonoma*), decorated with a simple "country-style" flower arrangement and a calligraphy scroll.

Above Not all tea ceremonies take place inside a tea house. A special lacquered table is prepared for an outdoor tea ceremony (*no-da-te*), often conducted in an informal style. Food, as well as whipped green tea, is offered to guests at most tea ceremonies

Right Planting in tea gardens is generally less tightly controlled and more suggestive of a wilderness. Glossy evergreen shrubs, such as camellias, aucubas, holly and mahonias, are planted in a more random fashion, but are still clipped to keep them from becoming too large.

Designing a tea garden

When you are creating a tea garden of your own, it could either be a simple affair with just a few scattered rocks, bamboos and natural paving and bamboo gates, or one with a much more studied look. Either way, a tea garden can include a range of decorative features as well as follow certain aesthetic rules. For example, it would normally include gates, water basins, lanterns and involve an attention to detail and cleanliness that is apparent in all Japanese gardens. The tea house itself could be quite traditional in appearance, built with a thatched roof and sliding panels. One shogun even had a portable tea house built that was gilded throughout, as a symbol of his power. Thus, the principles of the tea garden could be melded to suit the aspirations and taste of the owner.

Garden plan | A tea garden

The tea garden can be adapted to almost any garden. The main feature is the path of stepping stones inside the main gates that leads to the tea house via a waiting room, past lanterns and water basins, and through gates. The garden should become progressively wilder as the path approaches the tea house. This, as in so many of the Japanese arts, is achieved symbolically rather than literally.

How to construct a *tsukubai*

One of the most symbolic features of the Japanese garden is the *tsukubai*, a stone basin that is replenished with water, in which visitors wash their hands before entering the tea house. The basin is usually made from a hollowed-out rock, but any basin that is dignified enough, including a stone trough, could be used.

1 Choose a small, level site. The cobbles can extend as far as you wish, but the area need be no more than a circle with the diameter of the plastic dustbin (trash can).

2 Mark out the diameter of the dustbin and dig out a hole slightly wider and deeper than its dimensions. At the same time, dig out a saucer-shaped depression around the hole. When this depression is lined, it will allow any water blown from the basin to drain back into the reservoir.

3 Place a layer of sand at the bottom of the hole. Put the dustbin in the hole and check the rim is just lower than the depression. Check that the sides are level with a spirit level. If necessary, lift out the bin and adjust the base of the hole.

4 Backfill the gap between the bin and the hole sides with soil and ram firm with a piece of timber, such as a cut-down broom handle.

5 Rake the surrounding soil and remove any stones. Remove any soil from the bin.

6 Before lowering the submersible pump on to two bricks or a piece of broken paving, which will act as a plinth, attach a flexible delivery pipe to the pump outlet. Take the pipe over the side of the reservoir and push it through a rigid tube of bamboo, 60–90cm (2–3ft) tall, positioned next to the reservoir. Then, push the pipe through to a further bamboo tube positioned to spill into the basin. These *tsukubai* spouts are available ready-made from most good garden centres.

7 Lay the plastic sheet over the depression and over the dustbin and cut out a hole, 5cm (2in) smaller than the bin diameter.

8 Lay the galvanized metal grid or mesh, which should be larger than the diameter of the dustbin, over the plastic. Fill the dustbin with water.

9 Position the spill basin at the side of the grid, but make sure that it slightly overhangs the reservoir so that it will overflow on to the cobbles.

10 Test the flow of water, adjusting the regulator on the pump or moving the position of the spout so that the water falls into the saucer part of the spill basin. Arrange the cobbles over the metal grid.

Waiting room ①

Outer *roji*   Stepping stone path

④

Entrance gate

Above Guests rest in a waiting booth before the host invites them to the tea house itself.

Tea house

6

8

7

Lavatory

Tied rock

Bamboo
fence

5

9

Well

Inner *roji*

Moss

Moss

Rock

Lantern

3

2

Tsukubai

Plant list

1 *Enkianthus perulatus*

2 Clipped azalea

3 Autumn-flowering
   camellia (*Camellia
   sasanqua*)

4 Sedge (*Carex*)

5 Domestic bamboo
   (*Nandina domestica*)

6 Red pine (*Pinus
   densiflora*)

7 Japanese black pine
   (*Pinus thunbergii*)

8 Japanese maples
   (*Acer palmatum*)

9 Fern (*many species*)

Above A fence and gate along
the tea path divide the garden
into two halves.

Above The *tsukubai,* or "crouching
basin", is always accompanied by
a lantern.

Building a *tsukubai*

Hollowed-out basin stone
which overflows into grid

Metal grid over
polythene layer

Electric cable to pump

Brick plinth to support
pump above bottom

Shorter piece of
bamboo tube

Pipe inside
bamboo tube

Cobbles

Reservoir such as a
dustbin

Flexible pipe from pump

Stroll gardens

A stroll garden is one in which the visitor is encouraged to amble along paths that usually circle around a small pond or lake. Although there had been stroll gardens in Japan since the 14th century, they came to the fore in the Edo period of the 17th century and beyond.

Unlike the earlier pond and stream gardens, which were mostly used for boating, the stroll garden was a garden with paths that wove among a new set of garden motifs. Tea houses, tea arbours, lanterns, bridges, and contrived views of scenes reproduced from historic or famous places around Japan or even as far away as China, were carefully designed to entertain the stroller.

In most stroll gardens, rocks played a far less prominent role than they had in the Kamakura and Muromachi periods, partly because, in the Edo period, rocks were far scarcer around the new capital of Tokyo than they were around Kyoto. This scarcity led garden designers to rely more on clipped shrubs for dramatic form. This distinctive form of topiary is a fine art that is still practised

extensively today. All kinds of plants were clipped in a practice that was known as *o-karikomi*. Shrubs were trimmed into hedges or rounded forms like small hills. Sometimes, huge piles of evergreens were carved into abstract shapes. These mounds of clipped shrubs were made up mostly of azaleas and camellias, but any number of evergreens might be employed and, occasionally, deciduous shrubs such as enkianthus, which fire up red in the autumn.

When rocks were used, they might be strung in beads along the edge of ponds or used as stepping stones along paths or across inlets. Some of these stones were recycled architectural fragments such as temple pillar bases, old bridge supports or mill stones. This practice of recycling materials was known as *mitate* ("to see anew").

Opposite A mass of clipped azaleas is typical of the planting style in Edo period stroll gardens. A few rocks are interspersed among them, but rocks generally feature less prominently than in earlier styles.

Playful character

The pervasive aesthetic of the times was not as "spiritual" as that of the earlier dry and tea gardens. There was more of a sense of playfulness (*asobi*) as well as a desire for the sumptuous and magnificent. Japanese garden owners prided themselves on their connoisseurship of the arts. Nevertheless, many of these stroll gardens fell short of being overly ostentatious because they still employed the restraint and cultivated poverty of many of the aspects of the tea garden. This restraint in garden design was known as *shibumi* (meaning "astringent") due to their markedly minimalist, unpretentious and subdued beauty. *Shibumi* is a term that can also be used in order to describe many contemporary Japanese gardens.

Although some of the gardens of the *daimyos* (land-owning lords) were somewhat grandiose, there are others that were delightful and playful in their use of plants, water and architecture.

A stroll garden could be 50 acres (20 hectares) or be created in as little as a quarter of an acre (about 25 square metres). Through the careful use of space and weaving paths, smaller areas can be made to look much larger than they actually are. One device that was commonly practised by the Japanese was the borrowing of scenery, such as distant hills and castles, outside the bounds of the garden, a technique known as *shakkei*.

The stroll garden is one of the most familiar Japanese garden styles, partly because it incorporates so many aspects of other styles. Thus, you will find stepping-stone paths, lanterns, water basins and tea houses from the tea garden, as well as expanses of sand with a rock or two, usually near the main building, and the use of water as streams, waterfalls and ponds. Other elements might include bamboo fences and bridges of all kinds.

Romanticism

In the years following the fall of the Tokugawa shogunate at the end of the Edo period and the restoration of the emperor as head of state (Meiji period), there was a return to the more romantic ideals, as portrayed in the Heian period, 1,000 years earlier. Some

Below The 14th-century garden of the Tenryu-ji was one of the first pond-style gardens with strolling paths, but this was a period when the natural placement of rocks was the key feature.

Below Azaleas in flower in the small stroll garden at Shisendo, Kyoto. It is a simple garden with fine sand paths, rounded azaleas, and a small pool with irises. Clipping the azaleas reduces their flowering power.

Left An early Edo period stroll garden in Kyoto. Here the rocks are dramatic and symbolic of the power of the shogun, Tokugawa Ieyasu, who built this garden at Nijo Castle.

of these late-19th-century stroll gardens took on a more gentle naturalistic form, in which streams were designed like those found in the wooded mountains. This style might be more appealing to Western gardeners than the earlier very prim, trimmed stroll gardens.

Viewing points

Although stroll gardens are designed to be walked around, they are also meant to be viewed from the main house or from arbours in the garden. Traditional Japanese houses had verandahs, raised above ground-level, from which you might look over an expanse of brushed or raked sand stretching as far as the pond. Near the edge might be clipped azaleas and an occasional rock. Distant shores could be overhung by pines, their branches supported by posts. On promontories, a fine lantern might be chosen as a kind of lighthouse that would look attractive when covered in snow. There might be an island or two, or just a rock jutting out of the water.

Stroll-garden streams

At one end of the pond, a stream will enter, with a wide estuary traversed with stepping stones made from natural stone or formal slabs. Bridges that cross over streams or inlets might be made of a single slab of curved carved granite or be a curved wooden bridge, sometimes painted red like a Chinese bridge. In more naturalistic settings, log bridges or natural stone can be used. The stream would babble over pebbles as it entered the pond. Further upstream, it would be narrower, tumbling between rocks and over waterfalls, and hugged by ferns and sedges. If you are blessed with a natural fall of land, create a stream that follows the desires of the ground. If your garden is flat, then create the illusion of a mountain or hillside from which a stream might naturally flow. In most cases, you will need a pump to recycle the water, especially if your pond is stocked with fish, particularly koi and carp, but the water should be kept fairly shallow (about 60cm/2ft), so the fish can be easily seen. Deeper bays and shelters can be built to give the fish some shade and protection in the extreme heat or cold.

The route to the tea house

If a tea house is planned, the visitor will be drawn along paths of stepping stones, guided by bamboo fences and through gates, and past lanterns and water basins to the tea house itself. Tea arbours are more open than tea houses, as they were used for less formal occasions where visitors might be offered a commanding view of the garden. Other buildings might include a thatched umbrella shelter or a Chinese-style hexagonal summerhouse. Paths may pass through groves of cherries or maples, sometimes in an open grassy glade, under-carpeted with moss, where the shade is deeper.

Designing a stroll garden

Although stroll gardens incorporate many elements, rarely do the individual components distract from the whole. They can simply be a path, a pond, a few clipped shrubs, a lantern and some trees, such as maples, pines or cherries. There is no need to "decorate" the garden, as in the West. Even though stroll gardens may lack the spirituality of other garden styles, they obey certain rules of balance and look to nature or famous scenes for inspiration. When designing a garden in this style, concentrate on a well-shaped pond and an interesting path rather than a handful of "Japanese" artefacts and clipped shrubs.

Above The azaleas in the garden of Murin-an are clipped into abstract shapes and dispersed more randomly. On chalky gardens, where azaleas will not grow, boxwood and hollies could be clipped in much the same way.

Right A lantern sits on a promontory, playing the role of a lighthouse. Lanterns, in varied styles, are often strategically placed around the strolling paths, near gateways and at the base of hills. The flowering grass is *Miscanthus*, a native of Japan where it grows in waste ground.

Right The 19th-century garden of Murin-an
is full of illusions. A pair of wild-looking
mountain streams, which weave through
the grassy meadows and merge in the
foreground, appear almost like great rivers
flowing through the "hills" of azalea. The
whole garden seems vast because it borrows
the distant mountains as part of its design.
It is hard to believe that this small serene
garden, which effectively appears to be in the
heart of the countryside, is actually hemmed
in on three sides by busy city streets hidden
behind the walls and the ring of pines and
maples surrounding the garden.

Garden plan │ A stroll garden

A stroll garden can be made in a relatively small space. It will typically be centred around a small pond with a garden path weaving around it, which will stop at a Chinese-style arbour as a vantage point for features such as cherry groves, waterfalls, iris beds, a natural stone bridge and a wisteria-covered arbour. Plants may also be clipped to imitate distant hills.

How to construct a waterfall and stream

The design and construction of an informal stream and waterfall system offers endless opportunities. Although there are pre-formed stream units available, the use of a flexible liner and a variety of rocks contributes to a more natural-looking cascade in which the width of the stream and waterfalls will vary.

1 Mark out the direction and width of the stream with canes, identifying where any waterfalls will be positioned.

2 Dig out the stream to a depth of 20–23cm (8–9in) in a series of steps. Rake over and remove any sharp edges.

3 Starting from the marginal shelf in the bottom pool, drape the liner along the route of the stream, ensuring that there is enough to incorporate the vertical steps, and the sides where the liner will be tucked up behind rocks along the streamside.

4 With the liner loosely in place, put a foundation stone on the marginal shelf of the bottom pool to act as a support for a flat waterfall spillstone on top.

5 Make a fold in the liner behind the spillstone to prevent water from seeping under the stone. Place rocks at the side of the spillstone so that the water is directed over the flat stone. Mortar the gaps between the rocks to ensure a waterproof seal.

6 Place rocks either side of the stream, ensuring there is adequate liner outside the rocks so that it can be lifted into a vertical position above the waterline. Hold the edges of the liner in place with soil.

7 Repeat this process until you reach the stream top. Create a small pool to receive water from a buried pipe running from the pump.

Hexagonal thatched arbour

Clipped hedge

Stepping stone path

Plant list

1 *Iris ensata*
2 *Wisteria floribunda*
3 Clipped azalea
4 Weeping cherry trees (*Prunus subhirtella pendula*)
5 Japanese maple (*Acer palmatum*)
6 Bamboo
7 Red pine (*Pinus densiflora*)
8 Japanese black pine (*Pinus thunbergii*)

Building a stream and waterfall system

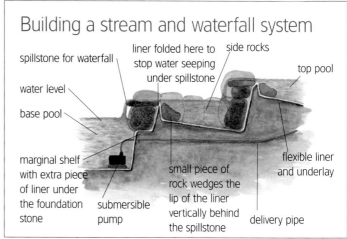

spillstone for waterfall

liner folded here to stop water seeping under spillstone

side rocks

top pool

water level

base pool

marginal shelf with extra piece of liner under the foundation stone

submersible pump

small piece of rock wedges the lip of the liner vertically behind the spillstone

flexible liner and underlay

delivery pipe

Cherry grove

Flowering wisteria arbour

② ④

Mixed hedge

Moss

⑤ ⑧

Waterfall

Carp stone

Pebble bottom

Rocks

③

Lantern on promontory

Millstone stepping stones

Water

Solid granite slab bridge

①

Yatsu-hashi bridge

Iris beds

Pond outlet

Hooped bamboo strips

Dry sand garden

Above Lanterns may be placed on promontories as the watchful symbol of a lighthouse.

Above Recycled materials (*mitate*) such as these millstones, make beautiful stepping stones.

Above Waterfalls and pond inlets in stroll gardens are built with naturalism and artistry.

Above There are many styles of bridge in wood or stone. A single slab of stone looks very natural.

Courtyard gardens

The history of the courtyard garden starts in the early 17th century, but for contemporary designers the small, enclosed space adjoining a building still offers fantastic design possibilities. Small courtyard gardens, designed to be viewed through glass panels or set within atriums open to the sky, are now being created in museums, corporate headquarters and homes.

In the Heian period courtyard gardens, or *tsubos*, were simple, small, enclosed spaces, perhaps inhabited by a single plant. The rooms that overlooked them, and the courtyards themselves, were named after these plants (for example paulownias or wisterias) and the Imperial Palace of Sento, in Kyoto, still has a Wisteria Court. Although the medieval residences of the samurai would have had *tsubos*, it was the rise of the merchant class in the late 16th century and throughout the

Edo period that led to the refinement of the art of the courtyard garden (*tsubo-niwa*) in the early 17th century. The small Edo courtyard gardens, like the much larger stroll gardens of the same period, are amalgams of preceding garden styles, but they often lacked the coherent principles and philosophies that lay behind their parent styles. Rarely, for instance, when the inspiration was a tea garden were tea paths actually used, nor did religion play a role. Instead courtyard gardens appropriated the motifs and

Left Courtyard-style gardens began in the 17th century. Courtyard gardens borrow motifs from other styles, such as the rocks and sand of the dry garden and the stepping-stone path of the tea garden. A lantern and bamboo give a vertical lift to the design.

Opposite This tiny garden at Sanzen-in is a welcome island of green in the centre of the building, where there is only just enough light for plants such as ferns, mosses and bamboos to grow.

artefacts of previous styles. Where, for example, it was not possible to build a tea house, a room in the house might be used. The journey to this room could be via a "path" (*roji*) that would lead guests there with a detour through the wilderness in the garden to maintain the illusion that they were heading somewhere special.

Hidden spaces

As the Edo period progressed, the insularity of the shogun's policies made the landed *daimyo* poorer, while the merchants accumulated great wealth. They were obviously unwilling and afraid to show it. Consequently, their modest shop fronts concealed a complex world of deep rooms and small enclosures, passages and courtyards hidden from the public in a style (*machiya*) that made economic use of space.

Through the use of sliding screens, small fence panels and bamboo blinds, it is possible to view these internal gardens from

Above An entrance garden to the Silver Pavilion illustrates the exceptional artistry of combining natural forms with the geometric. The bent red pine contrasts with the timber frame of the walls, while the diamond pattern of paving shows that the Japanese are not entirely shy of symmetry when it is called for.

different angles, each one framed within the rectilinear bounds of doors and window frames. The distinction between indoors and outdoors disappears. Westerners who were astonished by the stroll gardens when Japan was forced to open up in the mid-19th century, were equally amazed by these beautiful small town gardens.

The temple complexes also had *tsuboniwa* gardens, usually simple dry gardens with one or two rocks and a "pool" of raked gravel. So, too, did restaurants, where narrow passageways were made into elaborate gardens with stone paving bordered by lanterns and clipped evergreens such as azaleas, mahonias, nandinas and bamboos. These gardens were, and still are, invariably too shady and too small for broadleaf flowering shrubs or cherries, limiting the range of plants to glossy evergreen shrubs such as aucubas, fatsias and camellias, as well as shade-loving ferns, bamboos and farfugiums. There is also often a carpeting of moss, just as you would have found in a tea garden with its shady walks and scattered rocks.

The modern legacy

In many ways, the courtyard style – a hybrid between the dry garden and the tea garden – survives today, and is often highly refined. Some have everything from lanterns, water basins, small bridges, gravel and rocks to shady plants and sections of fencing used as a partition or to create privacy. Intricate journeys are hinted at, but are never more than that. Courtyard gardens are often today interpreted in a minimalist style, maybe simply a single clump of bamboo planted off-centre or a group of rocks with ferns and moss.

Roof gardens also need to be mentioned. The raw, open, soil-less space on top of a building is perfect for the dry-landscape treatment, particularly where there are any worries that excess weight from an abundance of plants, pots, soil and water might damage the building's structure. The use of sand, lightweight plants and even fibreglass rocks in the Japanese style is often the ideal solution to this.

Below Dry gardens can give surprising life to inner courtyards where few plants would grow. The great tsunamis of sand add a sense of movement in this garden at Ryogen-in.

Below Most Japanese gardens use a grey-white quartzite grit, but this modern garden uses red gravel. Mirei Shigemori designed this garden in the Tofuku-ji temple complex in the 1950s.

Garden plan | A courtyard garden

Tsubo-niwa, or courtyard gardens, can be made in the most unpromising sites, in narrow passages or in places where little light can reach. They often include elements from other garden styles, such as sand and rocks from the dry garden, or stepping-stone paths, lanterns and basins from the tea garden. Plants could include a clipped pine, an azalea, bamboo and a few ferns.

How to construct stepping stones

A Japanese stepping-stone path may use a mixture of natural stones, square-edged paving and recycled millstones. Depending on their size they are easy to install.

1 Measure the depth of the stepping stone. The stone should sit proud of the surrounding sand or moss by about 4–6cm (1½–2½in).

2 Dig out to a depth of 8-12cm (3–4½in) below where the underside of the stepping stone will be and refill with an aggregate base of around 6-8cm (2½–3in) deep.

3 Firm the base thoroughly before placing a layer of soft or sharp sand 2.5-4cm (1–1½in) deep.

4 Place the stepping stone down on to this layer of sand and, using a block of wood and a hammer, tap down on to the stone to firm it in place, being careful to avoid damaging the surface. Alternatively place a small amount of concrete around the stone (an 8:1 ratio of soft sand to cement) and leave it to set.

5 When the whole path has been laid, sprinkle sharp sand or small chippings over the whole area to a depth of 2.5-4cm (1–1½in) to finish your dry garden.

6 Weed-suppressing matting can be placed over the aggregate layer, but this will not prevent weeds from rooting into the upper sandy layers.

Glass

Above Sleeve fences are used to deflect or to help frame a view.

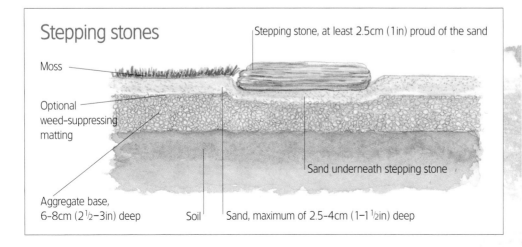

Stepping stones

Stepping stone, at least 2.5cm (1in) proud of the sand

Moss

Optional weed-suppressing matting

Aggregate base, 6-8cm (2½–3in) deep

Soil

Sand, maximum of 2.5-4cm (1–1½in) deep

Sand underneath stepping stone

Plant list

1 Clipped bamboo (*Phyllostachys nigra henonis*)

2 Soft shield fern (*Polystichum setiferum*)

3 Clipped azalea

4 Hart's tongue fern (*Asplenium scolopendrium*)

5 Red pine (*Pinus densiflora*)

Sleeve fence

Lantern

Bamboo fence

Large rock

Stone

Stepping stones

Mossy mound

Sand

Water basin

Step down

Verandah

Left Tall water basins (*chozubachi*) are often placed where they can be reached from the verandah. Long-handled ladles of metal or carved bamboo are usually laid across them, along with a bamboo lattice to prevent leaves from falling in.

Right Stepping stones across sand look effective when surrounded by moss. These paths may be used for tea ceremonies, where guests will leave the house by one door, and walk along the path and into a specially prepared tea room.

Elements of nature

There are a number of natural elements that form an essential vocabulary for the Japanese garden and this chapter looks at each of them: rocks, water and plants, and in dry gardens, sand, pebbles and gravel. The original Japanese word for landscape was *shan-shui*, meaning "mountain–water". Although dry gardens, by definition, do not include water, the element is central to most of the other garden styles as ponds, streams and waterfalls, or as simple basins.

Rocks were central to both Chinese and Japanese gardens as symbols of sacred mountains and islands, and they were also revered by the Shintoists. Rocks are given a kind of consciousness that guides the designer to follow their desires. This means developing an innate feeling for the best way to set them. Similarly designers apply these sentiments to the desires of water when creating a stream or waterfall for a landscape.

Opposite The careful placement of the rocks in this stream shows how the designer, Ogawa, has observed naturally formed rocky streams.

Above, from left Maples overhanging a pool at Murin-an; rocks in a quilt of moss; a toad lily (*Tricyrtis*) by a cobble-bottomed stream.

Although some dry gardens contain no plants at all, plants provide an important contribution to the Japanese garden, from plum trees and cherry blossom to spring-flowering shrubs, summer flower displays to the fiery reds of autumn and the bamboos and pines of winter.

In Zen dry gardens, natural elements are often used to replace others: sand is used to imitate water, for example, while some garden plants, such as azaleas, are used as substitutes for rocks. Dry water gardens frequently use moss, gravel, grass and sand. Moss grows profusely in Japan, a natural groundcover that allows more freedom with planting than grass. In Western gardens where lawns often dominate, plants are usually confined to borders or planted as specimens. Moss, on the other hand, enables the designer to position rocks, water and plants where he pleases.

Gravel, like moss, frees up the designer in the same way. Originally used in Japanese gardens as an open expanse for ceremonial occasions, in one great artistic leap in the 15th century gravel was employed by painter-gardeners to imitate the whiteness of canvas and as a substitute for water. These spaces also represented the emptiness of the mind, a goal of Zen meditation.

The use of the harsher edges of quarried rocks, concrete and, to a lesser degree, of plastics and fibreglass has given contemporary Japanese garden designers a new challenge. These new gardens often have a hard and dynamic edge, but the rawness of nature is still revered.

Above, from left A dwarf red pine clipped to look old and wizened; the waves of these two seas of sand seas "interrupt" each other; this mountain stream shows how Japan's landscape inspires its gardens.

Opposite A corner of the dry garden at Nanzen-ji shows how trees, rocks, moss, clipped shrubs and sand can be arranged with great simplicity. Achieving such harmony is far more difficult than it seems.

Rocks

These have formed the foundation of the Japanese garden from the earliest days. No other culture has made rocks so central to its garden art and, in consequence, no designer can now place rocks without wondering how a Japanese garden designer might set them.

While it may seem sensible to treat rocks and water separately, the two are frequently used togther in the garden. It is possible to trace the history of the placement of rocks, from their first use in shrines and later as motifs for sacred mountains to their grouping in and around water. Later, though, in the dry gardens of the Muromachi period (1393–1568), water was replaced by sand, while in the gardens of the Edo period (1603–1867) rocks were replaced by clipped shrubs, which were used to imitate hills and mountains.

Spiritual qualities and symbolism

Rocks were originally thought to possess spirits and the ability to draw the gods down to earth. They were later used to represent the mountain homes of the immortals, as well as the Buddha and his attendants. Zen monks, who had little time for superstition, rejected much of the esoteric symbolism of rocks and gave them more philosophic and painterly roles.

Although rocks were, and still are, placed in symbolic groups, they now tend to be arranged according to certain aesthetic rules. It takes a well-trained and experienced eye to read the symbolism in a group of stones. Groups of rocks that may appear entirely natural may actually possess a number of possible symbols. Therein lies the genius of the Japanese rock-setters. That does not mean you should not attempt to create symbolic arrangements in your own garden. Historians and Zen practitioners may like to read complex messages in classic rock arrangements, but it is not necessary to have such a deep understanding to compose successful groupings. It was, after all, the study of Chinese and Japanese minimalist ink-and-brush paintings that inspired them. Take a look at some of those paintings. The important thing to remember is that less is more and not to be too decorative in your approach. What you leave out is almost more important than what you put in, and neither the rocks and the gravel nor the plants need be fancy or remarkable in themselves.

Creating a rock garden

We are fortunate that the Japanese rated rocks so highly because we have a good idea of what ancient gardens looked like, making it possible to emulate the placement and grouping of the rocks in our own gardens. One garden in the city of Nara, 80km (50 miles) south of Kyoto, which was excavated in the 1970s, was found to be

Left The setting of rocks is the central creative dynamic in the making of most Japanese gardens. Even when used symbolically, the rocks are set in a way that is sympathetic to their natural desires.

over a thousand years old. There, the rocks are arranged in a surprisingly naturalistic way around a pond and stream, providing us with a useful example to follow.

Avoid using rocks with fantastic shapes, which have never been popular in Japan, except during a brief Edo/Confucian period. Chinese gardeners, in general, were much keener on fantastic sculptural rocks, many of them raised from the beds of lakes, standing them on pedestals as symbols of immortality. The Japanese, on the other hand, are more interested in discovering a rock's inner natural essence.

Above The scale and quantity of these rocks at Nijo Castle were intended to express the power of Ieyasu Tokugawa (1543–1616) in the early 1600s. The result creates potent imagery of a natural landscape.

When selecting rocks for a Japanese garden, choose ones that are interesting and quirky, but not too eccentric, and which can be partially buried. It is interesting to note that the rocks of the famous Ryoan-ji garden are not individually that remarkable; their hypnotic power lies in their arrangement, inspired by the way rocks and boulders can be seen poking out of the sea or a lake.

The genius of the rocks' placement was probably due to the instincts of the low-caste *karawamono* or "river men" who laid them out. Their technique of rock placement reflected their affinity with the way rocks lay in relation to water. The Ryoan-ji is a good source of inspiration if you are creating a dry-water garden and are looking for ideas for setting the rocks.

The most favoured rocks in Japanese gardens are often angular with either pointed or flattish tops. These shapes echo the angular strokes of a paintbrush, but such distinctive shapes also stand out well when viewed from a distance. When you are using rocks as symbols – perhaps to represent Mount Horai, Shimusen or Sanzon, the Buddhist Trinity, or crane and turtle islands, for example – make sure they are subtly arranged so that they have a quiet, still presence. If you have a fairly large garden, perhaps with a large pond or lake, you might also want to place special rocks for mooring boats or for creating bridges and grottoes. Stone is also the preferred material for making water basins. From a design point of view, there is endless scope when working with larger rocks, but don't get carried away with design ideas and remember the inner essence of the rocks if you wish to achieve a natural effect that does not jar with the rest of the setting.

Above At the Konchi-in, in Kyoto, the eye of the viewer is drawn to the rocks as they sit in the centre of a layered composition, with its foreground of raked sand and backdrop of evergreens.

Rocks are generally placed in groups. Seven was an auspicious number to the Chinese, as it is in many cultures, and was the original number of the Mystic Isles. Music was composed in units of 7-5-3 beats, while the prayers recited to Buddha Amida were chanted 7, 5 and 3 times in succession. By the 15th century, all kinds of objects were arranged in groups of 15, including rocks. The Ryoan-ji, for instance, is a 5-2-3-2-3 arrangement.

Most groups will consist of one main stone and up to five accessory stones, with one or more unifying stones to stabilize the group, while others might be used as linking stones to link together the members of one group, as well as different groups. The accessory stones can be placed to the front, rear or side of the main stone, huddled up against it or some distance away, but they should never obscure it. Also try making the attendant stones respond to or echo the angle or position of the main stone. These attendant stones are said to respond to the energy of the main stone in one of the following seven ways.

Receptive A rock that is placed to receive the energy from the main stone that is leaning towards it.

Transmitting An attendant rock that transmits energy from the main stone towards others in the group.

Pulling By angling this rock, it will counteract a main stone that leans away from it.

Pursuing Set behind a main stone that leans away from it, this rock is angled in the same direction, as if following it.

Stopping Where an upright main stone is stabilized by an accompanying one.

Attacking Where the accompanying rock leans towards a neutral, upright main stone.

Flowing This rock is a passive conductor rather than a more active transmitter; often flat, it acts as a kind of conduit to others.

These terms are not meant to be rigid, but they help to describe the relationship of the stones to each other and to clarify what might work in a particular grouping. They also highlight the subtle approach that is required to make such a grouping work. If a grouping does not look right, then work through these terms to help give the stones an authentic Japanese touch.

By far the best way of learning how to arrange rocks, however, is by studying good examples. Because of the static nature of rocks, it is possible to do this from photographs, but note that arrangements must look good from any angle, although they will tend to have one front side that gets the most attention. Also bear in mind that it is better not to simply copy an arrangement, but to be creative, seeking out and following the "desires" of the stone.

Top right Mount Horai is the tallest of the mythical Mystic Isles, often portrayed by the tallest rock, with others relating to it. Clipped azalea hedges (*o-karikomi*) add a curious but playful drama in the garden of Raikyu-ji, a masterpiece of the designer Kabori Enshu (early 1600s).

Middle right The central rock in this arrangement represents the Buddha, with two subservient attendant stones.

Bottom right The tall, flat-topped rock with its attendant rocks in the dry garden of Ryogen-in is thought to represent Mount Shimusen, a mountain at the centre of the Buddhist cosmology.

Ponds, streams and waterfalls

Streams have a history in Japan of being used on ceremonial occasions as settings for poetry readings and for drinking tea and saki. They would typically lead in and out of shallow ponds, often home to koi and the common carp. Ponds were also combined with small islands, and a pine on an island is one of the classic images of Japan. Waterfalls are the third water element, believed by Japanese gardeners to be best placed where they can reflect the moon. Water has a naturally mesmerizing quality and it is easy to understand the spiritual significance of its various incarnations in the Japanese garden.

Water around Kyoto, and throughout the mountainous regions of Japan, is abundant. The choice of Kyoto as the new capital in the 10th century was partly due to the way the hills frame the area, but also due to the south and westward flow of its rivers. In geomantic terms, the southward course towards the sun (fire) was said to bring life, growth and good fortune. While mountains were said to have a meditative quality, and were seen as symbols of the gods and the Buddha, water was a source of joy and detachment.

Ponds and streams

The first Japanese gardens of the Nara and early Heian periods possessed winding streams that bordered the main courtyard before feeding the main pond. Such streams were often bordered by rocks, the two forming an important relationship. An august stone might be used to mark the headwater of the stream as it entered the garden. Other rocks would "follow the request" of this stone, responding to its position and shape, forcing the water this way and that, changing its

mood as it approached the pond. Mountainside, torrent-style streams required the scattering of many more random stones causing the stream to divide and flow rapidly through narrowing channels.

A *yarimizu* is a meandering stream like the type that might be found flowing through a meadow, and it can be used in gardens to create a wetland area with a sedge-like estuary planted with reeds and irises. The stream's point of entry into this wetland should be indiscernible, and the water level should be kept fairly high, like a flooded estuary. These estuaries are often crossed by zig-zag, eight-plank bridges (*yatsuhashi*) that weave over iris beds or baskets of irises secured to the stream or pond bed.

Opposite The arrangement of the rocks, the laying of the shingle beach and the pruning of the trees at Syoko-ho-en, in Kyoto, has been achieved with such artistry that the hand of the artist is hidden. You could be forgiven for believing that you are in the mountains instead of in the middle of Kyoto.

Right A dramatic waterfall in the Japanese gardens in Portland, Oregon, in the United States, is viewed from the *yatsuhashi*-style bridge that staggers through beds of water irises.

Waterfalls

These are another essential feature of pond and stream gardens and stroll gardens. They are often built to represent the Buddhist Trinity, with one large stone at the centre, over which the water tumbles, supported on either side by two attendant stones that stand slightly further forward. Large and important waterfalls were often known as dragon-gate waterfalls after the Chinese symbol for waterfall, which included both a dragon and water.

A stone might be placed at a waterfall's base to represent a carp, as if it were about to leap. This "carp stone" symbolized spiritual and mental effort in Buddhist and Confucian terms. The carp, symbolically, would change into a dragon on reaching the top of the waterfall. The carp stone points to the strivings of an individual to better himself.

Pond shape and design

Whether by stream or waterfall, the water will eventually tumble into a pond. In Japanese gardens, ponds tend to be no deeper than 45cm (18in), so that they are easily kept clean and clear, and the fish can be seen. Try to include a stream flowing out of the pond because these are said to carry away evil spirits. When planting the pond with lotuses (*Nelumbo*) or water lilies (*Nymphaea*), make sure that the growth does not become too choked or the pond may silt up after a few years.

The proposed design of the pond edges will determine what happens to the water. For example, the water might appear to lap against a rocky shoreline, with a few solitary stones jutting out into the water, or become a wide inlet bordered by a sand bar. One sand-bar scene − the Aminoshidate peninsula in western Honshu − is so famous that it is one of the three most important landscapes in Japan. It is often symbolically reproduced in Japanese gardens, often shown with a lantern on a promontory to represent a lighthouse.

The shapes of ponds should, if possible, recall a natural scene, perhaps even the seaside. One ancient nobleman had his serfs boil seaweed to remind him of his childhood home by the sea.

Below A thin stream of water falls on to a flat stone, creating a louder sound and making a more decorative pattern than if it had simply fallen into a pool of water.

Below A carp stone at the base of a waterfall in the gardens of the Golden Pavilion. The carp stone signifies the strivings of the individual who is transformed into a dragon upon reaching the top.

The edges of ponds can be supported by rocks or timber posts. If you are using a pond liner, make sure that the liner is hidden by edging stones, timbers or plants. Occasionally, ponds can be given the shape of an ideogram symbolizing the heart, water or a gourd, or can even be loosely outlined in the image of a turtle or crane. It is more common, though, to find turtles and cranes in the shape of an island of the Mystic Isles.

Island styles

The use of islands in Japanese gardens might reproduce special scenes, such as the hundreds of extraordinary rocky islets in Matsushima Bay, near Sendai, in northern Honshu. Some of these islands are very small, but most have some kind of plant life, mostly pines, growing in their rocky crevices. The pine is a resilient tree that can take on fantastic forms as it is buffeted by salty winds. The Japanese expend an enormous effort pruning to give garden pines this characteristically wizened and windswept look.

Above One of the shallow upper pools in the garden of Murin-an. The pool is punctuated by islands of sedge, bordered by mossy banks with ferns and overhung with maples.

Apart from the pine-covered island, there are other island styles, including the Rocky Islet and Cove Beach Island, all of which are described in the *Sakuteiki*. The Meadow Isle is made up of low rocks, moss and autumn grasses. Forest Isles have random trees and grass, while Cloud and Mist Islands have sandy beaches planted in a spare, wispy way. These styles can be recreated in your Japanese garden by growing suitable plants so as to set an atmospheric scene.

Islands were originally placed towards the middle of the pond, but slightly off-centre, to create a sense of mystery so that, whether boating or walking, you might find an inlet, grotto, waterfall, or even another island behind them. Try to maintain this element of surprise if you are designing a pond with islands.

Right This is a quintessential and perfectly enchanting Japanese garden at Hosen–in, Ohara. An open walkway passes by the garden, with stone steps leading down to a patch of gravel. Stepping stones traverse the pool, which is surrounded by clipped azaleas and one clipped *Enkianthus*, turning burnt red in the background. In the foreground, the vertical leaf-stems of *Equisetum hyemale* contrast with the rounded forms of the azaleas. Of the larger trees, the nearest is a Japanese maple (*Acer palmatum*) in full autumn dress, leaning over the pool, while behind it a *Stewartia*, with its patchwork bark, has a slightly more muted colour. In the back right is a large, white-flowered *Camellia sasanqua*, which typically flowers in the autumn.

Dry water

The original dry landscape gardens focused on the placement of rocks in moss or grass. In later dry gardens rocks were set in sand, gravel and among pebbles, with these elements arranged and spread to imitate the qualities of water.

The first two great gardens that used rocks set in moss or grass were the Saiho-ji, or Moss Temple, and Tenryu-ji, dating back to the 14th century. At the Tenryu-ji there is a superb example of a dry waterfall, known as the Dragon Gate Waterfall, created with all the power of a real waterfall. At the Saiho-ji, there is a large representation of a turtle, and a hillside set with dramatic arrangements of rocks.

The Zen monks who created such dry gardens realized that the imagination is more captivated by a suggestion than by reality.

Or, as they might have put it, the power of the imagined shape yields a far greater truth than one locked up in the real. This is what is meant by the poetic term *yugen,* or "the spirit of hidden depth".

Streams, as opposed to still water, are portrayed in their "dry" form by the use of river-washed pebbles laid out carefully in overlapping patterns to indicate a sense of flow. The image is completed by the use of a few larger boulders or rocks, as well as bridges made of large stone slabs.

Opposite The dry garden of Shoden-ji uses clipped azaleas instead of rocks. The azaleas are planted in the same 5-3-2-5 arrangement that was used for placing rocks in 15th- and 16th-century temple gardens.

The best sand to use in dry gardens is a large, greyish-white quartzite grit. If it is too white, then the glare from the sun can be too dazzling. The lightness of colour is especially effective in moonlight, when shadows are cast on the alternating lines of the raked "waves". These waves change from straight lines into concentric circles as they ripple against and lap around the groups of rocks. The raking of sand is not only part of the design, but also a part of the daily meditation of the Zen monks and gardeners. Specially designed 1m (3½ft) wide wooden, toothed rakes, similar to a hay rake, draw the sand into ridges, often leaving slightly higher ones at the edges. Lighter sand in gardens, such as those at Shisendo, in Kyoto, can also be brushed with birch-twig brooms.

Modern designers often use a dry rock-and-sand garden to create even more abstract patterns, using quarry-blasted rocks rather than naturally occurring weathered stones. This takes the "suggestive" nature of the dry landscape into the realm of contemporary design. If you are careful with the composition, space and balance of the layout, these gardens can be very successful, and fairly easy to manage. Not all modern Japanese garden designers follow Zen precepts, but they have become more Western in outlook. However, the overall look is still very Japanese.

Top At Tofukuji, the 20th-century artist-designer Mirei Shigemori used sand to imitate water, recalling ocean waves lapping at island shores.

Above Waves ripple on the surface of a platform raised from the surrounding area in the dry garden of the 15th-century Ginkakuji, or Silver Pavilion. The platform may have been added in the 18th century.

Left One of the original dry-style gardens was the waterless Dragon Gate Waterfall created in the 14th century at Tenryu-ji.

Plants

Ever since the early days, plants have played symbolic, religious, romantic and poetic roles in Japanese gardens. Apart from the dry garden, other gardens are usually planted with at least one pine, or a bamboo, plum, cherry, azalea or maple.

Although Japan's mountains, streams and coastlines are brimming with superb flora, the disciplined restraint of Japanese gardens employs a limited range of plants. The native plant area in Kyoto's botanical garden is full of plants that Western gardens would relish, but most of them would not find a home in a Japanese garden.

The problem with many Western imitations of Japanese gardens is that designers cannot resist using all those attractive Japanese plants that would not normally be used; for example, those that are considered too colourful or are the wrong shape. However, this restraint does not mean that the Japanese do not appreciate plants. On the contrary, the Japanese celebrate flowers a great deal, perhaps more than any other nation, especially those that signify a change in the seasons or that are associated with certain festivals. As the last snows melt, the plum trees (or Japanese apricots) start wafting out their scent and are celebrated with a quiet reverence. The cherry

blossom season then attracts thousands to gardens with the best displays, with parties gathering under their boughs. Although there are a number of native, later spring-flowering shrubs — for example, some deutzias, spiraeas and kerrias — they all play second fiddle to the cherries, wisterias, peonies, azaleas and camellias.

The summer begins with a show of irises that grow in swampy ground at the heads of ponds, and in pots as prized and cosseted specimens. Hollyhocks (*Alcea rosea*), hydrangeas, the lotus (*Nelumbo*) and the morning glory (*Ipomoea*) are all cultivated by the Japanese to keep the season going. Many plants cultivated in different climates do not grow well in the hot, wet Japanese summers, but will revive in the spring and autumn.

Autumn maples (*Acer*) are as important as the spring cherries in the Japanese floral calendar. Their fiery reds contrast with the deep greens of the evergreen pines and the fleeting blossom of the autumn-flowering camellia (*Camellia sasanqua*). Lespedeza, platycodon, toad lilies (*Tricyrtis*) and farfugium all add extra interest.

The most favoured plants for winter interest are bamboos and pines, which can withstand the cold. Snow-covered pines also make a beautiful sight. Japan is also blessed with an exceptional number of evergreen shrubs that thrive in its acidic soil and temperate climate.

Left The glorious sight of cascading branches festooned with blossom is the highlight of the Japanese floral calendar, with festive celebrations going on well into the night.

Opposite A patchwork of different species of moss in the dappled sunshine at Sanzen-in, Ohara, near Kyoto. The soft velvet carpets of moss under a silent stand of Japanese cedars (*Cryptomeria*) produce an effect that may be difficult to reproduce in climates other than that of Japan, where it grows profusely.

Planting styles

Most shrubs in the Japanese garden are set out in random, natural-looking groups or as individual specimens. Formal styles are rarely used, and you will not see shrubs and flowers planted for their textural or colourful effects as in a typical Western garden. In tea gardens, you will find plants such as ferns that lend a wild quality to the design. In stark contrast, other gardens are planted with clipped evergreens. This look is at its most artistic in the 17th-century art of *o-karikomi*, in which groups of shrubs, usually azaleas and camellias, are clipped into abstract topiary shapes.

Hedges are another important feature for which a great miscellany of shrubs can be used. While some hedges look fairly uniform from a distance, they may actually contain as many as 20 or more species from a list including *Elaeagnus*, *Pieris*, *Camellia*, *Azalea*, *Ficus*, *Aucuba*, *Osmanthus* and *Nandina*.

The Japanese garden is by no means devoid of colour and scent. Town gardens might include hydrangeas, hollyhocks, sweet peas (*Lathyrus odorata*), morning glories and anything from a clematis to an azalea growing in pots outside the door. This planting effect is something that would be simple to create in any small city garden.

Opposite A pagoda-style lantern provides the central focus of the entire garden at Sanzen-in. The mixed hedge curves up a hillside of randomly placed, clipped azaleas. This kind of topiary in Japan is known as *o-karikomi*.

Right Azaleas, ferns and moss surround a stone well-head in a private garden in Ohara. The multi-stemmed conifer at the back right that has been clipped into layers is a Hinoki cypress (*Chamaecyparis obtusa*), a native forest tree of Japan.

Below right A dwarf form of the soft-needled female pine or Japanese red pine (*Pinus densiflora*) emerges from an island of moss, before a backdrop of the peerless mixed tones of the autumn leaves of maples (*Acer palmatum*).

Moss and grass

An important ingredient in most Japanese gardens, moss requires the right balance of sun and shade in order to grow well. In Kyoto, for example, it will grow virtually anywhere because of the high rainfall during the summer.

The variety of different species of moss gives the surface of the garden a beautiful, velvety texture in all shades of green, often highlighted by the dappled sun if the moss is growing beneath trees. However, bear in mind that, while moss is an attractive feature when it is used to carpet part of the garden, it does need to be cared for and weeded to keep in shape.

The advantage of growing moss over grass is that it gives the Japanese designer much more freedom in terms of positioning plants because moss does not need to be mown in the same way as grass. Rocks can also be positioned without the constraints placed on gardens in which grass is the main foundation. If you are not blessed with a climate in which moss grows freely, you can easily improvise by using a ground-cover of mondo grass (*Ophiopogon*) or perhaps some shorn bamboos.

Grass is rarely used as ground-cover in the Japanese garden except in very large gardens, where the drought-resistant *Zoyza* grass can be planted. This deep-rooting grass is not mown tight to the ground, and left at a height of approximately 8cm (3in). However, this grass turns brown in the winter. Grass on banks and between rocks is trimmed and clipped as neatly as in a Western garden.

Creative constructs

A common impression of the Japanese garden is that it is decked out with lanterns, curved red bridges, basins and bamboo fences. Designing a Japanese garden, however, is not simply about assembling these familiar Japanese artefacts along with a few clipped azaleas, a bent pine and a bamboo, and then expecting a good result. You may, in fact, be able to create a more authentic atmosphere without any of these, especially if you understand the aesthetic principles behind the Japanese garden. These man-made constructs add form and scale to a garden and, when used well, can contribute to its beauty. There are hundreds of designs for fences, lanterns and water basins, for example. Such objects are not placed as sculpture is in Western gardens, but blended to be an intrinsic part of the whole composition.

Opposite This understated composition at Koto-in, Kyoto, illustrates just how little is needed to conjure a perfectly serene atmosphere.

Above, from left A bamboo fence; a stone bridge spanning a pond; a water basin filling from a water pipe hidden inside tubes of bamboo.

The Japanese garden designer is deeply absorbed in the energy of natural materials, choosing them very carefully so that he can blend them beautifully into the design of the garden. Most fences and garden buildings are built of raw timber, bamboo, sisal and reeds, exhibiting the spectacular quality of those materials, while lanterns and water basins are often carved out of the finest stone and encouraged to weather.

Paths, like fences, are also designed with great care and creativity. Natural and formally cut slabs and granite setts, old millstones, cobbles, sand and gravel are combined using a balance of man's deliberate artistry with nature's own perfection. Bridges, apart from those that are painted red in the Chinese style, are often made of timber or of simple, curved slabs of chiselled granite.

The sequence of these man-made constructs follows a logical pattern. As we enter the garden, we will pass through a gate and will be aware of the fences that frame the garden and lead us onwards. Paths, especially in the tea garden, will show us the route. Lanterns are placed strategically to light the way, while water basins are placed near to tea houses to purify the hands and mouth. The destination of many paths is the tea house or an arbour with a great prospect over the garden. Understanding this process will help the budding Japanese garden designer to place them with more thoughtfulness.

Above, from left A water basin in a private garden in Ohara; the tops of bamboo fence posts; stepping stones through a Japanese garden, with roof tiles dividing two kinds of gravel.

Opposite Statues of the Buddha are not common in Japanese gardens, but this one makes up part of an entrancing collection assembled in a forest of bamboo by the early 20th-century artist Hashimoto Kansetsu.

Boundaries

Ever since Heian times (AD 785–1184), when Kyoto was laid out on a strict grid system, Japanese gardens have invariably had distinctive boundaries. This approach did not really change until the Edo period (1603–1867) when gardens became large enough for their perimeters to be of secondary importance to the overall design.

Walls

The outer boundary walls of large houses and temple gardens in the pre-Edo period were designed as an expresssion of the architecture of the buildings. They also became an important backdrop and could be seen from within the garden. These boundary walls were often built of clay and tiles, and were neatly plastered. With a stout wooden framework and bracket as a cornice, they were usually crowned with ornamental tiling, although they were sometimes thatched on the top with a ridge of protective tiles.

These walls were rather grand structures, suited to palaces and temples, but smaller residences used many of the same techniques and materials. Modern materials of brick and stone were used more rarely in traditional Japanese gardens, although many garden boundaries on slopes were supported by stone retaining walls, sometimes with azaleas growing in their crevices. Incidentally, internal walls around courtyards were often lower than perimeter walls, so giving views of trees or distant hills. In both large and small Japanese gardens, walls are not used as they are in Western gardens for growing exotic plants or fruits. When climbing plants are grown, for example, they are allowed to twine through light bamboo trellising.

Fences

Beyond the practicalities of privacy and security, fences were, and still are, considered an important garden feature. In the use of bamboo, in particular, the Japanese have excelled in their inventiveness. Sometimes woven into wonderful patterns, bundled together, tied with jute, or combined with branches, twigs, thatch or bundles of reeds, the ornate bamboo fence might simply flow alongside a path or help to direct the way.

Left The wall surrounding the garden amidst the sweeping roofs of the temple of Tofuku-ji is an intrinsic part of the overall design, with its vertical blackened timber supports and its heavily tiled coping.

Opposite Fences are positioned strategically within gardens to divide them into parts, to draw the visitor onwards and to seduce and deflect the eye, as in this private garden designed by Marc Keane.

Right This is quite an aggressive style of bamboo fence with sharpened points protecting the roots of the pine from wandering feet in the public space outside Nijo castle.

Below left Vertical bands of reeds seem to mimic the trunks of the trees in the elegant bamboo fence in Nanzen-in.

Below right There are hundreds of designs of fence to choose from, many dating back to the Kamakura period (the 13th century), where the attention to detail extends to every tie and binding.

Hedges of Japanese box (*Buxus microphyllus*), evergreen oak (*Quercus*), Japanese cedar (*Cryptomeria*), *Photinia* and *Podocarpus* are also very common. Where they thin near their base, however, they may be backed by bamboo fencing.

In general, most timber fences are left raw and unpainted. At their most rustic, planks might be old and weathered or deliberately chiselled and charred to give an instantly aged effect.

A hybrid between a fence and a wall is the wattle-and-daub fence. The upright support timbers are often left exposed and stained black. Posts with horizontal, vertical or even angled boarding are also used, sometimes with the boards staggered to allow air and light through and occasionally with gaps that are wide enough to allow visitors to peep out.

Gates

These were most popular in tea gardens, developing their most elaborate and ritualistic style by the early 17th century. To design a tea garden today, it is advisable to follow the traditional layout that has been so successful for centuries. The tea garden is often divided into two or even three parts: an inner, middle and outer garden, or *roji*, with specially designed gates opening into each area.

The main entrance gate (*roji-mon*) may be a large tile-covered gatehouse or a simple thatch-covered bamboo gate. The second gate into the middle or inner *roji* might be a small crawl-through opening or stooping gate (*naka-kuguri*). One type has a door that is hinged at the top so that the guest has to push it forward and up to get through, being forced to bow in the process. The tea host might prop open this hanging gate with a bamboo pole before inviting the guests to follow him into the tea house. This middle gate is seen as a pivotal point in the journey along the tea path. Through the act of "crawling", the guest leaves behind the material world for a more spiritual and sacred realm. In many tea gardens, especially small ones, a low portal or post may be all there is to suggest an inner gate, but many guests will grasp its

Right Brushwood, reeds, timber posts and bamboo are all combined in this sleeve fence, which stands at the corner of a house and helps to divide up the garden.

significance. You might not wish to go to these lengths in your own garden, but creating a series of sections, each with their own entrance, will enhance the feeling of deference as you approach the tea house proper, and give your garden an air of authenticity.

The entrance to the traditional tea house was through a small, sliding-door hatch (*nijiri-guchi*) at floor level, so that the only way to enter was on your hands and knees. Even emperors and shoguns had to enter this way, one of the few moments in their lives where they had to meet others on an equal footing.

Sleeve fences (*sode-gaki*)

These are screens of bamboo and reeds that were, and still are, used for two reasons: to deflect the view to another part of the garden, and to create privacy. This is especially true in restaurants, where guests do not want to be aware of others, yet wish to look at the same garden, usually a courtyard (*tsuboniwa*). About 2m (6½ft) high by 1m (3½ft) wide, often curved at the shoulder and pierced by an aperture, sleeve fences come in different designs and work well in modern gardens.

Paths

Japanese garden paths have evolved from the simple surfaces of gravel and fine sand that were originally used for paths circling around ponds, to the stepping-stone paths of the tea garden where each step carries spiritual significance for the traveller. Similarly, some of the path styles are simple and naturalistic whereas others use highly sophisticated materials and designs.

Path materials

By the Kamakura period (1185–1392), when the first stroll gardens were constructed, garden paths were likely to have been laid with a mixture of compacted fine sand and a light grit surface, similar to the one used for ceremonies in the courtyards of Heian residences, both materials readily available today. Although gravel paths need maintenance, they provide one of the easiest and cheapest means of providing an all-weather surface in gardens, particularly in rainy climates such as Japan's. The paths need to be occasionally topped up with fresh gravel, weeded and then brushed with bamboo brooms.

Gravel is a loose material that must be contained within solid edges. Path edges use paving or cobbles, as well as old roofing tiles, long strips of chiselled granite or charred post tops, always with great sensitivity. The path itself might be made with randomly arranged paving or cobbling. The joints between the paving or cobbling are filled with compacted sharp sand, usually rapidly colonized by moss. If the moss is uncontrolled in favourable climates it can swell up and almost envelop the surface; this is not always discouraged, because moss is both natural and beautiful. While moss is not really meant for walking on, many paths do become soft and mossy and perfect as a surface on which to wander.

Opposite Dramatic changes in the angles of paths encourage the stroller to take in new views. This path at Koto-in combines the formal with the informal, its random paving stones bordered by long rectangular strips of granite.

Right A simple rustic path of random paving leads through informal shrubs and past an iron lantern placed on a stone on its journey to a thatched tea room.

Design and direction

The purpose of paths in the Japanese garden is to control the experience of the stroller, with each change of direction introducing a new view. From the earliest times, paths have suddenly stopped or turned abruptly, a device that encourages the stroller to hesitate and scan a view that has been deliberately composed to be seen from a particular spot. Zig-zag paths and bridges take this idea to a greater extreme.

Paths found their true calling in the tea garden and were originally known as dewy paths (*roji*). The tea path recalls the pilgrimages that sages, painters and Zen monks made on their

visits to China in search of renowned artists and sages, who lived, often in exile, in huts and hermitages in the hills and mountains. As the tea guest is drawn along the *roji*, he is made more conscious of each step he takes through the use of stepping stones. These had previously only been used to cross water and swampy, muddy ground. Their addition to the tea garden was initiated by Rikyu, one of the great tea masters of the 16th century. The strategic placement of some larger stepping stones on a path gives the visitor the freedom to be less conscious of where his feet are falling and so look up or cleanse himself at a water basin. Stepping stones were also kept scrupulously clean, brushed and even damped down to give the impression of mountain dew. Damping down was also a welcoming gesture towards guests.

During the 16th century, as the tea ceremony and garden evolved to an ever higher aesthetic importance in the lives of the merchants and samurai, so too did the style of tea paths. In their early manifestations, the paths were wilder, lending more emphasis to the rugged, but under the influence of later tea masters, stepping stone paths became more "artistic" and elaborate.

Different path styles – *Shin-gyo-so*

The fashion for idiosyncratic artistry in garden paths allows designers to use a variety of materials and patterns. If the original tea paths were laid out with a series of informal (*so*), natural slabs of stone or buried boulders, later contemporary paths blend in more formal (*shin*) shapes. Formal paths may be made of square paving, bordered by long, rectangular granite setts, or paved in random but rectilinear patterns, in the same way as most Western garden terraces. Rectangular or square paving might also be set out in a staggered line through plants or across a sea of sand. Other paths might be semi-formal (*gyo*) where the square forms are mixed with informal cobbles, roofing tiles set on edge, and natural paving. The use of old roof tiles, mill stones and reclaimed relics from old buildings is considered a sign of good taste.

Left The formality of this path cutting through the dry garden of Tenju-an is softened by an enveloping carpet of moss. The path takes a sudden right-angle turn at the end. The pine is a black pine (*Pinus thunbergii*).

Stepping-stone paths were, and still are, designed to unite separate parts of a garden, often with quite different atmospheres. The path may, for example, start near to the house, being set with formal paving or cobbling, and then launch off across a sea of sand before entering a more earthy and mossy "forest" area planted with maples and shrubs.

In some Japanese gardens, especially dry ones (*kare-sansui*) – which were mostly designed to be viewed from one particular place, such as the verandah of a building – the paths of stepping stones might be set to weave right across the garden. In the past, these paths were rarely taken, but were rather used by the garden designers of the day to suggest

Above Small stepping stones sunk in a lush carpet of moss wander through this private garden in Ohara. The small symbolic "lantern" at the base of the tree is made of stones piled one on top of the other.

movement and to draw the viewer's eye across a particular scene. If a path was not supposed to be taken, for reasons of privacy or in order to delay the tea guests from entering the inner tea garden, a small, round boulder that was bound with a knotted string, rather like a small parcel, would be left in the middle of a paving stone. This would indicate to any visitors to the garden that the path was not yet meant to be used for crossing the space.

Bridges

Always a dominant feature, bridges tend to be associated with Japanese gardens. One of the original styles was the Chinese-style bridge that was lavishly ornamented, high-arched and lacquered red. As the islands represented the abodes of the Immortals, bridges symbolized the crossing over to that world. Red-painted bridges (*sori-hashi*) are often closely associated with Japanese gardens, but they are generally more rare than those made of more natural materials and unpainted wood.

In the garden of the Tenryu-ji, built in the 14th century, a Chinese-style, curved, red wooden bridge was replaced by a series of flat, natural-stone slabs, propped up on rock pillars. Later gardens used single pieces of wrought granite, supported by granite piles. Some of these granite slabs were carved with a gentle curve. This was the dominant style of Japanese bridge until Chinese high-arched bridges made a return in the Edo period (1603–1867). These semicircular bridges, known as full-moon bridges because their reflections make up a complete circle, are so steep that the only way to cross over them is by means of steps going up one side and then down the other.

Below A good example of a *yatsu-hashi* bridge of planks, resting on wooden piles, staggers past baskets of irises towards an impressive stand of cycads on the far bank.

Yatsu-hashi

Especially designed for viewing iris beds, the *yatsuhashi*-style of bridge, which is still popular today, is constructed from a series of single horizontal planks supported by short wooden piles driven into the mud at the head of the pond, where the Japanese love to grow beds of irises. The planks crisscross the swampy beds in a zigzag fashion, forcing the visitor to loiter, watch the fish and admire the flowers. This simple style of bridge can be easily incorporated into today's Japanese garden, perhaps designed with a boggy area in which moisture-lovers such as irises and sedges can be grown.

Below A moss-covered log bridge in the famous gardens of Saiho-ji, the Moss temple in Kyoto, where over 60 species of moss are said to grow. The path is more to suggest a journey than to be used.

Right This massive curving slab of schist in the grounds of Nijo castle is a potent symbol of strength. The original garden was thought to have been designed as a dry garden with no water at all.

Below right This stepping-stone bridge in the garden of Tenju-an is made of unusually shaped piers, possibly recycled temple-pillar bases.

Wattle and log bridges

Bridges were also made from wattle covered in earth or from batches of logs bundled and laid across a timber frame, which were then covered with earth and gravel. These bridges were designed more for effect than for use because they were fairly fragile, and did not usually feature a hand-rail. Those that link up the islands at the famous Moss Temple, in Kyoto, for example, are quite rotten, but they blend in perfectly with the deep shady mystery of the garden. If you wish to construct a bridge such as this in your own garden, then bear in mind how long the bridge will last and whether the logs should be treated first to improve their longevity. Nowadays, wattle is not readily available, so it is best to use bundles of logs that have been coated in a wood preservative, or a good hardwood, such as oak, which needs no treatment.

Wisteria bridges

Sturdy wooden bridges with a trellised canopy designed to carry twining wisterias are popular, a style of bridge that was immortalized by Monet in his garden at Giverny, in France. The effect of the long racemes of the Japanese wisteria (*W. floribunda*) is doubled when they are reflected in the water. The cascades of wisteria flowers create a shady, scented walkway across the water.

Stepping-stone bridges

This style of bridge is also popular, whether it is made of recycled pillars or natural rocks. Like the *yatsu-hashi*, the stones stagger across the water instead of taking a straight line, offering a variety of views as you cross streams, inlets and ponds. If you are lucky enough to have a large garden in the country with an expanse of water, then this would make a delightful feature, enticing visitors to cross the water and so to view the garden from different angles.

Lanterns

Stone lanterns are one of the most distinctive sculptural artefacts in the Japanese garden. Originally these lanterns stood outside Shinto shrines and Buddhist temples. Princes and nobles donated lanterns as votive offerings to the shrines. They stood in their hundreds around some shrines, sometimes lined up in avenues on either side of the path.

Lanterns found their way into the Japanese garden, like many other artefacts such as the water basin and the stepping-stone path, by way of the tea garden. Lanterns were originally placed to illuminate tea paths and water basins, as many tea gatherings were arranged in the evening. They were also placed near pond edges to evoke lighthouses, at the base of hills or near wells. However, despite their popularity, stone lanterns (with oil and wick lamps or candles placed inside) never gave off that much light and were, to a large extent, ornamental.

Sculpted ornaments are rare in Japanese gardens, so the stone lantern, especially those made of granite, gives designers an opportunity to create something interesting and distinctive. Though granite lanterns take many years before they weather and age, instant antiquity can be given by smearing them with yoghurt or manure that promotes the growth of algae. Some Japanese gardeners even used the slime of crushed snails to achieve this effect. Stone artefacts also age more quickly in shade, and those made of more porous material, such as sandstone, sprout moss more readily.

Lanterns play such a large part in Japanese gardens that long ago they were classified into different types. Some were named after famous tea masters or gardens, while others were designed to look beautiful in snow. Although most lanterns were made of stone, some were wooden or thatched, while hanging lanterns might be made of bronze.

A classic arrangement consists of a lantern placed near a water basin, with one or two rocks and pebbles at the base, a backing piece of bamboo fence, and a pine or maple to provide shade and promote the growth of moss. This scene, which is considered a complete image, is suitable for a courtyard or entrance garden.

In a contemporary Japanese garden, electric lighting can be used very effectively, but great care must be taken to hide the fittings and wires so that they are not visible during the day, as this would rather spoil the romantic effect.

Left In some Japanese gardens, lanterns are the only architectural artefacts to be found. Most are never lit, but this one is. Rice-paper panels diffuse the light from the lit oiled paper.

Above left This lantern has been placed in the water in a garden in England. Lanterns set near or in the water represent lighthouses.

Above centre A lantern makes a strong statement among the stems of pines and maples in the Japanese garden at Portland, Oregon. Lanterns traditionally stood outside Buddhist and Shinto shrines.

Above right The introduction of the stone lantern into Japanese gardens came through the development of the tea garden, where they were used to light the path (*roji*) and water basins.

Below Lanterns were often designed to look dramatic – this one is majestically placed within a pond.

Water basins

Outside every Shinto shrine, and most Buddhist temples, there are water basins with bamboo ladles or scoops so that visitors can cleanse their hands, face and mouth. Water is an important part of the Shinto religion, being a means of physical and spiritual purification.

Zen Buddhism promoted cleanliness to help create an awareness of inner purity and, as has been emphasized elsewhere, the outer and inner world of Zen is constantly reflected in motifs throughout Japan's garden history, particularly in the tea garden. In fact, you will rarely find a Japanese garden that does not have a water basin of some kind. Some are filled from a surreptitious bamboo pipe that, if allowed to drip, will keep the water fresh, rippling and constantly overflowing. This means that guests need a special stone to stand on that does not get wet, while extra pebbles are required to help the overflow drain away.

Types of water basin

Although water basins come in all shapes and sizes, in cut and natural stone, ceramic and wood, there are essentially two types.

Chozubachi-type basins are usually up to 1m (3½ft) high and are placed on verandahs where they can be easily reached. These basins may also have a slatted bamboo cover to prevent leaves and debris from falling in. The *tsukubai chozubachi* is a lower "crouching basin", placed on or just off the path to the tea house. The act of crouching, as with the crawl-through gate and the tea house's hatch-like entrance, compels the guest to humble himself. One famous anecdote recalls how the great tea master, Rikyu, gave visitors the only view from his tea garden of the beautiful Inland Sea at the moment they bowed before the *tsukubai*.

There are often special stone arrangements around the basin, featuring worn, rounded cobbles and pebbles, with accompanying stones, a lantern, ferns and evergreen shrubs. This grouping is, in many cases, all that has been found in old tea gardens, and is often reproduced in modern courtyard gardens (*tsuboniwa*).

When looking for water basins for your own garden, the natural stone kind is not easy to find and can be expensive. Pottery or stone urns make good alternatives. As with paths, *mitate* (recycled material) is another option, such as hollow, second-hand architectural pillars or old stupas.

Far left An elegant water basin in an English garden. Water basins are often filled constantly by fresh water, the excess draining away among rocks and pebbles. A sump could be built under the stones to collect the water, which can then be recycled using a submersible pump.

Left A 17th-century crouching basin (*tsukubai*) in the temple garden of the Ryoan-ji, with an inscription that means "I learn only to be contented", an important goal of Zen philosophy.

Top right Two water basins (*chozubachi*) that can be reached from the verandah of Sanzen-in, in Ohara. These types are square basins set on stone pillars.

Centre right The bowl of this basin in the Seiryu tea garden at Nijo castle garden is carved from a beautiful natural rock into the shape of a gourd, a symbol of hospitality.

Bottom right Ladles are laid over or by the side of the basin supported by a rack of bamboo. Tea guests use these to cleanse their hands, mouths and faces before entering the teahouse, as an act of physical and symbolic purification.

Buildings and arbours

Early Japanese gardens had Chinese-style, pond–and–garden viewing pavilions, often built at the end of a long covered corridor that was open to the sides. The introduction in the 16th century of the unique Japanese tea house would come to influence the style and character of Japanese garden buildings to the present day.

The tea house was originally conceived as "a mountain place in the city", often built as a rustic hut thatched with grass, but became increasingly sophisticated in design. The tea house was the place to which the tea garden path led, a place of reverence and social intercourse; it was not a place from which to view the garden. By the 17th century, especially in the exquisite gardens of the Katsura Palace, in Kyoto, the tea house opened up its sides and front to look out over the new pond and stroll gardens.

If you want to build a tea house in your garden, then you can create a structure that can be used as an outdoor room, but still retains an air of venerability. Close attention to the design and building materials will give your tea house an air of authenticity.

Tea house design and construction

In the past, tea houses, tea arbours and pavilions were made from a mixture of natural raw materials blended with finely planed, high-quality timber, with a floor consisting of a matrix of straw mats (*tatami*) bordered by fabric.

The supports for the buildings might be made using the whole trunks of small trees with the bark left on. The walls were often finished with plaster, lined with bound bamboo strips, or painted in muted, weathered gold and pale blue. These materials are all still readily available today, and you may be able to find a suitable garden designer or builder who can create a fairly realistic structure for you.

Opposite Two hermitage-style tea houses set side by side in the gardens of Tojo-in, Kyoto. The simple architecture and thatched roofs are modelled on those of rustic farm buildings. Although in a country style, they are often beautifully crafted, using only the best materials.

Right Wisteria-covered arbours are popular in Japanese gardens. They are simple constructions of robust timbers to carry the weighty stems of wisteria, with very little, if any, ornamentation.

Tea house interiors

The entrance to the 16th-century tea house was through a small 76cm (2¹⁄₂ft) square, sliding-door hatch, so that guests were forced to enter on their knees and demonstrate a suitable level of respect. Other window-like openings were often round, like the moon, or rectilinear with sliding, rice-paper panels. A sunken hearth for heating the tea water was placed off-centre, while in the special alcove (*tokonoma*) in the back wall would hang calligraphic scrolls. There might also be a vase containing a simple, seasonal, "country-style" flower arrangement. There was nothing ostentatious whatsoever about these tea houses, enabling them to blend beautifully into the landscape.

You may not wish to go to the trouble of building a sunken hearth in your tea house, but, even if you are simply using the tea house as an outdoor shelter or gazebo, you might still include some classic Japanese design features to give the structure an air of authenticity.

Other buildings

These might include a small, open-fronted waiting room, similar to a rustic shelter with benches, where guests can relax before being invited by the host to proceed to the teahouse. Tea gardens even have outside toilets built in a similar style to that of the teahouse.

In stroll gardens, raised boarded walkways for viewing the cherry blossom might terminate in a thatched pavilion. The Japanese gardens may also be viewed from under umbrella-shaped arbours, with a single pillar supporting a circular, or square, thatched roof. Some later Japanese gardens, which were influenced again by Chinese imports, had Chinese-style hexagonal buildings, similar to modern, Western gazebos. In and around such a shelter were often portable benches and tables, some in the style of Chinese porcelain tubs. These arbours were often placed in more prominent places than tea houses, for example on a hill crest or another vantage point.

In some ancient gardens, the contrast of bright red, paper umbrellas set over tables draped in red cloth, against dark green evergreen trees and shrubs, can be quite startling, an approach that would even suit a contemporary Japanese garden.

Left A waiting booth (*koshikake*) in the inner tea garden, or *roji*, at Chishaku-in, Kyoto. The stepping-stone paths lead into the simple shelter and then away from it through the bamboo gate towards the tea house itself.

Decorative artefacts

The addition of artful objects is generally avoided in Japanese gardens. The garden is regarded as a completely integrated composition, and the introduction of features can destroy the unity of the design. As many Japanese garden designs are either inspired by nature or reproduce famous views, they require few distractions that might divert the eye from reading the composition as a whole.

In the Japanese garden specimen plants, focal points, sculptures and statues are usually avoided, as are overt colour schemes, textural combinations, surprise effects and most of the elements that are the bedrock of many Western gardens. This is an important point because, when we come across garden stupas, pagodas, water basins and lanterns, or images of the Buddha, we

are in fact dealing with sculpted forms, some of which had obvious religious connotations. Although these artefacts are still integral to 21st-century Japanese gardens, their religious significance is often less weighted, with far more emphasis, for example, being placed on the way in which a pagoda might offer a strong vertical accent to the garden design.

Below A pagoda stands in the middle of an island in the gardens of the Golden Pavilion (Kinkaku-ji), in Kyoto. A felled tree acts as a bridge to the island.

Below Wells are often found in tea gardens, with a stone placed to the side on which to rest the water bucket. Many of them, like this one in Ohara, are purely ornamental and not functional.

Above Pagodas, Buddhist structures that evolved from Indian stupas, make arresting sights in gardens with their strong vertical accent. They are best placed when partially hidden among trees and shrubs.

Above right Carved reliefs and sculptures of the Buddha are sometimes placed in gardens, as many gardens are inspired by the philosophy of Zen Buddhism. Their presence gives an air of reverence and peace.

Pagodas and stupas

These are structures of the Buddhist treasure houses where relics and scriptures were stored to commemorate a saint. Like lanterns, they were originally found close to temples, but when used in the garden they do not dominate because they are such familiar images that they readily blend into the scene. Indeed, they represent a very recognizable feature, from a Western viewpoint, of the Japanese garden and what it should contain.

Other devices

There are one or two playful devices found in Japanese gardens that appear to recall a distant rural past. Deer scarers (*shishi odoshi*) are the best-known of these. They create a regular clacking sound as a bamboo tube fills up with water, tips over to overflow and, on its return, smacks against a rock.

A more unusual device is the *tsui kin kitsu*, where water drips through a narrow hole in the ground into a saucer at the bottom of a hollow underground chamber. When you listen to the dripping sound down a long, hollowed-out bamboo tube, you can hear an echo of waterfalls and streams in distant mountains, in much the same way that the wind in a conch reproduces the sounds of ocean waves.

Wells may also be found in gardens, constructed of timber or natural stone, often with a bamboo rack as a cover in order to prevent leaves from falling in.

Plant directory

The Japanese have planted beautiful trees and shrubs ever since they first started making gardens. Although many of these plants were brought over from China, the Japanese soon started planting many of their own native plants. Japan has exceptional and enviable native flora, including many species of cherry, azaleas, camellias and magnolias, which grow in the mountains. In the autumn, the maples and oaks give a display of fiery reds, yellows and oranges.

From the first plum blossom to the fading grasses of autumn and the snow-covered pine trees of winter, Japanese plants have been celebrated by poets and at pagan and religious festivals. Evergreen trees, such as cedars and pines, are considered symbols of longevity and resilience.

Opposite In the autumn the leaves of the Japanese maple (*Acer palmatum*) turn an amazing mixture of flame tones.

Above, from left The katsura tree (*Cercidiphyllum japonicum*); pot-grown chrysanthemums; a flowering cherry tree (*Prunus hillieri*).

Wisterias, peonies and hydrangeas feature in many Japanese gardens, but none are planted in flower borders. As a general rule, plants are placed in natural groupings or massed in orchard-like groves, such as cherries and plums. Herbaceous and bulbous plants, such as platycodons, lilies, hostas or Japanese anemones, are usually planted naturalistically with ferns in individual clumps near the base of a rock, in a carpet of moss, or scattered in small groups. Irises are planted in swampy areas or in formal beds near the inlet of ponds, while sedges and ferns are used to soften the edges of streams.

Some flowers are set aside for displaying in pots. Lilies, irises, chrysanthemums and even lotus plants are grown with intense care in beautiful pots that may be placed against woven bamboo screens.

Pruning is a specialized art. Gardeners clip pine trees into different shapes to evoke the old, weather-beaten and windswept trees that grow along the coast or to expose layered branches. Azaleas, camellias and other evergreen shrubs may be clipped into mounds, abstract shapes or more formal shapes. This reduces the number of flowers that plants such as azaleas will produce.

Due to the inspiration of monochrome paintings colour is less prominent in Japanese gardens, especially in Zen temple gardens and tea gardens – here colour is viewed as a distraction that destroys the simplicity of the design. But even in the simple, plantless, dry rock garden of the Ryoan-ji, plants are never completely absent, as the backdrop behind the wall is of cherries and maples that add seasonal colour.

Above, from left A maple native to Japan (*Acer shirasawanum*); the coral-barked *Acer palmatum* "Sango-kaku"; *Camellia sasanqua*.

Opposite Whole flower heads of *Camellia japonica* fall, scattering themselves over the forest floor and the gateway to a wooded shrine.

Spring trees and shrubs

The first signs of spring are a cause for celebration throughout the temperate world, no less so than in Japan. The azalea and the camellia are both evergreen; they lend themselves well to being clipped, and some varieties flower very early. Kerria has been grown in Japanese gardens since the 11th century and often flowers early, as do many species of Magnolia, some of which are native to Japan.

Camellia japonica
Tsubaki

This evergreen shrub, native to the warm temperate coasts of Japan, was planted in gardens together with species and hybrids from China. *Camellia sasanqua* has smaller, narrower leaves than *C. japonica*, and the pale pink single flowers appear sporadically through winter before dropping when spent.

Camellias are now common, but in the past they were found only in Buddhist temples. The simpler, paler coloured, single-flowered forms with glossy foliage, known as *wabi-suke*, were planted in tea gardens. Two types of camellia can be grown as hedges: the dense, glossy foliage of *C. japonica* or the tea plant *C. sinensis*, with smaller leaves than

other species and white flowers in autumn, often clipped to give a compact, dense shape.

Flowering time mid- to late spring
Size shrub or small tree to 9m (29^1/$_2$ft); keep to 2m (6^1/$_2$ft) by restricting the roots in a tub, or by regular stem pruning
Pruning by thinning out stems after flowering
Conditions light shade and away from early morning sun; moist, acid soil
Fully hardy/Z 6–7

Chaenomeles japonica
Boke

The Japanese quince is loved for its early flowers, which range in colour from the deepest scarlet to pale pink and white. They appear

before the leaves, clustered close to the bare, spiny stems. They can be pot grown, when they tend to take on a wizened habit of growth.
Flowering time spring
Size shrub to 1m (3ft)
Pruning by cutting back hard after flowering to encourage a compact habit, or train against a frame or wall
Conditions sun or partial shade; well-drained, slightly acid soil
Fully hardy/Z 5–8

Kerria japonica
Yamabuki

A deciduous shrub native to Japan, the kerria, or Jew's mallow, has been used in gardens since the 11th century. Its simple, five-petalled, orange-yellow, star-like flowers are a welcome sight in spring. Although

there are double-flowered forms and one with variegated leaves, Japanese gardens tend to use the single form, usually planted as part of a broader scheme.
Flowering time mid- to late spring
Size shrub to 2m (6^1/$_2$ft)
Pruning by thinning out old stems after flowering
Conditions full sun or partial shade; any soil
Fully hardy/Z 5–9

Magnolia
Mokuren

Native magnolias have been planted down the centuries and include the deep purple-pink, lily-flowered *Magnolia liliflora*, known as *mokuren*, the familiar white, star-flowered *M. stellata*,

hime-kobushi, and its taller close relative *M. kobus*, *kobushi*. The large *M. obovata* , to 15m (50ft), is a hardy, deciduous tree with highly scented, cream-coloured flowers in midsummer. In more recent years the bold American evergreen species, *M. grandiflora* (bull bay), growing to 18m (60ft), has proved popular with its large, creamy coloured flowers appearing in late summer. Magnolias are usually planted in large stroll gardens.

Flowering time mid-spring to midsummer

Size large shrub or small tree to 3-12m (10-40ft)

Pruning by removing over-long shoots in late winter

Conditions partial shade; rich, acid soil

Fully hardy/Z 5–9

Paulownia tomentosa

Although strictly a native of China, foxglove trees have been cultivated in Japan since the 9th century. Planted as specimen trees in the courtyards of the aristocrats, they became a symbol of the military leader, Hideyoshi. Paulownias have

two notable features: the fabulously large leaves and the beautiful, lavender-blue, foxglove-shaped flowers. It may take a few years and some mild winters before a paulownia will establish a strong stem, but once a trunk has been developed, the tree will form a handsome perfectly hardy crown.

Alternatively, the stems may be coppiced in spring to encourage the production of massive leaves, up to 30cm (12in) long. This eliminates the flowers, but, when combined with bamboos, palms and cycads, gives a bold, tropical feel.

Flowering time mid- to late spring

Size tree to 12m (40ft)

Pruning none needed unless grown as a pollard

Conditions sheltered position in full sun; any soil

Fully hardy/Z 6–9

Rhododendron (Azalea)
Satsuki (small-leaved);
Hi-rado (large-leaved)

Evergreen and deciduous azaleas belong to the genus *Rhododendron*

(*Tsutsuji*), of which 50 species are native to Japan. The two main kinds of azalea are the *kirishima* (*R. obtusum* type) and the slightly later flowering *satsuki* (*R. indicum*). There is also the large-leaved azalea, called *hirado*. Most of the thousand or more hybrids are of mixed parentage and have flowers that span the spectrum from purple through pink, to white and salmon. Flower sizes vary, as does the growth.

Azaleas, most of which flower after the cherries and wisterias, have no symbolic significance in the Japanese garden. *Kirishima* azaleas have been grown in gardens since the 11th century, though you'll often see them on treeless mountain sides in drifts and mounds. This natural habit has made azaleas the perfect subject for clipping for centuries; they lend themselves to being rounded into mounds that imitate hills, being trimmed down to echo the shape of a stream or being used in a clipped form with rocks, or at the edge of small pools, to add shape and contrast. The clipping also reduces the

Opposite and above, left to right

Camellia japonica; Chaenomeles japonica, the Japanese quince; *Kerria japonica*; scented flowers of *Magnolia stellata*; the young leaves of *Paulownia tomentosa*; azaleas clipped so that only a few flowers manage to open.

number of flowers, which, to the Japanese, is a bonus because too much colour over-stimulates the senses. Left unclipped, their flowering is so profuse that the leaves are completely obscured.

The art of *o-karikomi* (similar to the representational forms of topiary) is often practised on blocks of azaleas and camellias. In the garden at Shoden-ji, three groups of clipped azaleas have been planted as part of a dry landscape (*kare-sansui*).

Flowering time spring to early summer

Size shrub 1-3m (3-10ft)

Prune by shaping after flowering and, if necessary, again in the autumn

Conditions full sun or shade; moist, acid soil

Fully hardy/Z 6–9

Spring blossom

The end of winter is signalled by the plum blossom (*mume*) whose flowers, appearing as the last snows melt, are regarded as brave and resilient. The delicate pink flowers of the peach tree (*momo*) are the next to open after the plum, but it is for the *sakura,* or cherry blossom, that Japanese gardens have become famous the world over – their first flowers bring people out in celebration.

Prunus mume
No-ume

Like the European sloe (*Prunus spinosa*) and the damson (*P. damascena*), the deciduous Japanese plum (or, more correctly, Japanese apricot) has a pure white blossom, which may open in some areas while snow is still on the ground. The earliness of the blossom makes it one of the most popular flowers in Japan. The flowers of some forms are pale or deep pink, turning whole valleys into a haze of colour. The round fruit is often pickled or candied.

Unlike cherry trees, which are relatively short-lived and resent being pruned, venerable old plum trees may be pruned hard.

Old trees with their branches covered in lichen are revered more than vigorous young trees; the gnarled trunks might need to be propped up and bandaged like an old soldier, with ropes, jute and hessian, and should then still bear a few branches.

The festivals of plum-blossom viewing lack the boisterous aspect that you often find later in spring under the boughs of cherry blossom. Plum blossom is viewed when the weather is often quite cold and with quiet solemnity, touched with a hint of sadness. A symbol of purity and hope, it is revered as the prophet of spring. *Prunus mume* is also seen as the epitome of integrity and fidelity, "as virtuous as a true gentleman", and its resilience marks it out as one of the "three excellent plants" that bear the winter so bravely (the others are pine and bamboo). It was also said to be a courageous tree, releasing its scent from leafless branches while there was still the

Left Japanese plum blossom, *Prunus mume.*

last of the winter cold, which is why it was popular with warriors who might carry sprigs of it into battle. According to Japanese legend, when a warbler (the equivalent of a nightingale) sings in the branches of the plum, the two join together to become the spirit of the awakening spring.

The most common variety of *Prunus mume* in cultivation in Western gardens is the deep pink form called 'Beni Chidori', which is sweetly scented. It is an upright shrub to 3m (10ft). The variety 'Omoi-no-mama' is white. Suitable substitutes for damsons include *P. cerasifera* (cherry plum, myrobalan), which grows to 10m (30ft) and has white flowers in early spring (but avoid the purple-leaved form, 'Nigra'); *P. cerasifera* 'Princess' is suitable for a small garden. *P. glandulosa* is a shrub, to 1.5m (5ft), with white to pale pink flowers followed by red fruit.

Flowering time early spring
Size small tree to 9m (28½ft)
Pruning by thinning out old stems after flowering
Conditions full sun; any soil
Fully hardy/Z 7–9

Prunus persica
Momo

The deciduous Japanese peach is the next flowering tree, after the plum, to be honoured. Peaches were planted in great numbers on the sides of Kyoto's Momo-yama (Peach Mountain) as an emblem of longevity and perfection. It was on this same mountain that the great shogun Hideyoshi built his Fushimi castle in the late 1500s; his reign was later referred to as Momoyama.

Peach blossom is a soft, vibrant pink, and the flowers appear just as the leaves unfurl. The peach was thought to win over the spirits of the dead and was also a sign of new life. Concoctions of peach were taken at the first sign of pregnancy and were administered as a cure for morning sickness. Peach blossom festivals, originating in China, are still celebrated at the beginning of March. They are a special favourite among children, especially girls, who decorate themselves and their dolls in silk and lacquer and parade.

Peach trees are generally rather short lived (as little as 15 years) and are prey to a number of pests, including the disfiguring peach leaf curl.

Flowering time early spring
Size tree to 8m (25ft)
Pruning by removing dead, diseased and damaged branches in midsummer
Conditions full sun; rich, well-drained soil
Fully hardy/Z 7–9

Prunus serrulata
Sakura

When cherry trees start flowering, people take holidays, and there are huge spring celebrations for three weeks in April attended by thousands. Up and down the length of Japan, "The Land of the Cherry Blossom", friends gather in gardens and public parks to have picnics and sip sake well into the night, as the ephemeral clouds of blossom float above them. People also tie red paper lanterns in the branches, while children run around in the early evening, clapping to the music of drums and the lute-like *shamisens*.

The classic Japanese cherries mostly date from the late 19th-century Meiji period. These trees often have fully double and profuse blossoms that derive from the Japanese hill cherry, *Prunus serrulata* (oriental cherry). The best loved of its forms are those with white flowers with dark, unfurling leaves that are revealed as the petals fall. Many of these are grown in Western gardens, including *P*. 'Ukon' and *P*. 'Shogetsu'.

Before the 19th century Japanese gardens grew the species *P. incisa* (Fuji cherry) and *P. serrulata*, and their more subtle elegance was in keeping with the aesthetics of the times. They were also the object of veneration and celebration, their short-lived blossom being viewed by the samurai as a reminder of their own fragile mortality. They also regarded the cherry tree as a symbol of chivalry and loyalty to their lords and masters.

The first of the cherries to flower, from autumn to spring, is *P*. x *subhirtella* (Higan cherry, rosebud cherry). Its weeping forms, 'Pendula Rosea' and 'Pendula Rosea Plena', are very popular in Japan, the cascading branches propped up by cedar poles and bamboo frames. *P. incisa* flowers soon after, before the leaves appear; it makes a spreading, attractive tree to 8m (25ft).

Above, left to right *Prunus mume* varies in colour from deep pink to white; a weeping cherry; the Yoshino cherry, *P*. x *yedoensis*.

The next to flower is the hybrid *P*. x *yedoensis* (Yoshino cherry), which is named after Mount Yoshino. The white flowers appear before the leaves, and the spreading tree has a lovely, weeping form, 'Shidare-yoshino'. Around the Arishyama district of Kyoto and the gardens of the Tenryu-ji hundreds of Yoshino cherries have been planted and admired for over 800 years.

There are also innumerable forms of the hill cherry that are worth growing, such as *P. serrulata* 'Shirofugen', 'Shirotae' or 'Taihaku' and *P. jamasakura*. Some of these and other cherries, such as *P. sargentii* (Sargent cherry) and *P. incisa*, also have good but not flamboyant autumn colours.

Flowering time early spring
Size tree to 3-8m (10-25ft)
Pruning by removing dead, diseased and damaged branches in midsummer
Conditions full sun; rich, well-drained soil
Fully hardy/Z 7–9

Late spring and summer trees, shrubs and climbers

As the last of the cherry blossom falls, the wisteria unravels its pendulous, perfumed flowers. Alongside the wisteria, the tree peony unfurls its fabulous frilly petals, a plant treated with high regard by the Chinese long before the Japanese introduced it to their gardens.

Deutzia
Unohana, utsuki

As with spiraeas, the Japanese grow many species and forms of deutzia, or Japanese snowflower, in mixed plantings. The shrub's white or pink flowers are borne later than those of other spring-flowering shrubs and can be used to bridge the gap before the summer. *Deutzia crenata* and *D. gracilis*, both native to Japan, have clusters of star-shaped white flowers.
Flowering time late spring to early summer
Size shrub 1m (3ft)
Pruning by cutting out old flowering stems after flowering
Conditions full sun; any reasonable soil
Fully hardy/Z 5–9

Paeonia suffruticosa
Botan, moutan

The tree peony flowers at exactly the same time as the wisteria, and both are associated with beautiful women. There are many cultivars of *Paeonia suffruticosa*, known as the "flower of prosperity" and the "king of flowers" because of its luxuriant flowers. It is not easy to cultivate in Japan, and the flowers are rather too gorgeous and blowsy for the subtle refinement of most of their gardens, so it is usually grown in pots. The prized colours are white, pale pink and red. It is often represented on painted screens with lions, tigers and bamboos.
Flowering time late spring to early summer
Size shrub to 2.1m (7ft)
Pruning by removing over-long and crossing shoots in late winter
Conditions full sun or partial shade; deep, rich soil
Fully hardy/Z 4–8

Spiraea nipponica

Several species of spiraea are native to Japan, and most are small to medium-size shrubs. They tend

Above and left top to bottom
Wisteria floribunda; Chinese tree peony, *Paeonia suffruticosa*; a pink variety of the Japanese snowflower, *Deutzia*.

to round or spreading shrubs, with arching growth, decked with bunches of tiny flowers. *Spiraea nipponica* has dark green leaves and white flowers.
Flowering time midsummer
Size shrub to 1.2m (4ft)
Pruning by cutting hard back after flowering to remove old flowering stems
Conditions full sun; any soil
Fully hardy/Z 5–9

Stewartia pseudocamellia

Grown for its small, white-cupped, camellia-shaped flowers and mottled bark and autumn tints, this small to medium-size tree is often planted among mixed blocks of evergreen shrubs and occasionally as a specimen near a gateway.

Flowering time midsummer
Size tree to 20m (66ft)
Pruning none needed
Conditions full sun or light shade; moist, acid soil
Fully hardy/Z 5–7

Styrax japonicus

The Japanese snowbell is a broad, small deciduous tree, with glossy, dark green leaves and masses of small white flowers.
Flowering time early to midsummer
Size tree to 10m (30ft)
Pruning none needed
Conditions full sun or partial shade; moist, neutral to acid soil
Fully hardy/Z 6–8

Wisteria floribunda
Fuji

As soon as the cherry blossom has fallen in mid-spring, the long racemes of wisteria start to unravel. *Wisteria floribunda* is native to Japan, where it can be seen in the wild, tumbling out of tall trees and creating blue cascades on steep hillsides. *W. floribunda* has much longer racemes than its cousin from China, *W. sinensis*, and in the cultivar 'Macrobotrys' (formerly 'Multijuga') the racemes of lilac-blue flowers can reach 1.2m (4ft) long.

Wisterias were revered for their longevity and were the only climbing plants to have been seriously cultivated in Japanese gardens. They have been grown into pines since the 1600s, but they have been more often planted on frames, arbours and tripods. Wisterias also look terrific when they are draped over a specially constructed bridge, the long racemes reaching down to the water beneath to meet their reflection. Another wisteria grown in Japan is *W. brachybotrys* 'Shiro-kapitan' (syn. *W. venusta*), which produces attractive, beautifully scented white flowers a few weeks before the leaves appear.

Wisterias may also be trained against a firm stake as standards to stand alone as specimens. They also can be grown more as a shrub, by simply allowing them to grow along the ground. In order to keep wisterias within bounds, they need to be pruned quite hard. Pruning is done in two sessions, the first in midsummer, when long wands of growth are reduced by two-thirds, and the second in midwinter, when growth is further reduced to 10cm (4in) long spurs. The plants' tolerance of pruning has made them a subject for pot growing and bonsai treatment.
Flowering time early summer
Size to 9m (29½ft)
Pruning see above
Conditions full sun or partial shade; rich, moist soil
Fully hardy/Z 4–10

Above, from left *Stewartia japonica* has a wonderful patchwork bark; Wisteria is a classic plant of both Chinese and Japanese gardens.

Spring foliage

Early spring is not just about flowers. Japanese gardens often disdain too much colour. *Salix babylonica* (weeping willow) has been planted around ponds and lakes in Japan since its introduction from China in the 9th century. The soft green of its unfurling leaves is admired. The young foliage of *Acer palmatum* is quite varied with tints ranging from soft green to salmon pink. In general, purple, golden, and variegated foliage is not found in traditional gardens, because the colours are too unnatural and distracting from the overall design.

Summer flowers

Few flowers endure the summer rains in Japan as well as the hydrangea, and in recent years it has gained in popularity. Two flowers have been Buddhist symbols of mortality and immortality: the morning glory for its fleeting existence and the lotus, a symbol of purity as it emerges out of the mud. Also planted in muddy pools is the iris, a plant celebrated for its power to ward off evil spirits.

Hydrangea
Ajisai

Hydrangeas were first mentioned in Japanese gardens as early as AD759, but they never really caught on. The four petals and rather gloomy purple colours were felt to represent death. The common name, *ajisai*, means "to gather purple". They were also called *shichihenge*, which meant to change seven times, alluding to the way in which the flower colour changes through the season.

Three of the most important species of hydrangea are native to Japan, *Hydrangea macrophylla*, *H. petiolaris* (climbing hydrangea) and *H. serrata*. The great round mophead hybrids originated here and are found in a number of gardens. Among their attributes are their late-summer flowering and their ability to withstand heavy summer downpours. On acid soil with plenty of moisture, the blue varieties are intensely blue. The lacecaps, which come closer to the species in their flower form, are also very elegant and suitable for planting in light woodland shade. They are said to look best in the background of shady groves, where their mysterious beauty can be almost bewitching, especially when the flowers are moist from the rain. Varieties of *H. macrophylla* can also be grown in pots, if regularly fed and watered. The other species that is native to Japan is *H. paniculata*, which has cone-shaped flowerheads in late summer. It is ultra-hardy and can be grown in full sun.

All these hydrangeas come in a multitude of forms to suit every taste, and they have become very popular in Japan in recent years, with some towns and districts making the hydrangea their special flower.

Flowering time mid- to late summer

Size shrub to 2m (6¹/₂ft)

Pruning by removing dead and over-long shoots in early spring

Conditions sun or partial shade; moist, rich soil. Fully hardy/Z 4–9

Left The mop-headed *Hydrangea macrophylla* growing profusely in a shaded woodland.

Ipomoea
Asagao

During the Nara and Heian periods, when poets sang of the fleeting condition of human life, they latched on to morning glory as an ideal symbol: as one flower fades, it's quickly replaced by another. But it was in the 18th century that the morning glory became fashionable among the *daimyos*, who helped to create a new array of colours. In the 1830s another great revival occurred, which has since spread to almost every household. The morning glory was grown in pots over lightweight bamboo trellises and fences. Whereas so many flowers wilt at the onset of summer, the morning glory revels in the heat.

Flowering time summer to autumn

Size climber to 6m (20ft)

Conditions full sun; any soil Tender/Z 8–10

Iris
Hana-shobu

The iris is a great favourite in Japan. *Iris laevigata*, known as *kakitsubata*, grows naturally in the swamps around the ancient capital of Nara, where it was collected as a dye, its blue colour exclusively used to decorate the robes of the imperial family. In *The Pillow Book*, a novel dating from the 11th century, the author writes of the iris festival when men, women and children warded off evil spirits by adorning their hair and clothes with iris flowers and roots. The festival still takes place in late May and early June.

I. laevigata is cultivated in gardens in swampy, but not waterlogged, ground, often near an inlet to a pond. *Yatsuhashi* or zigzag plank bridges weave over the beds, forcing the visitor to slow down and admire the plants from different angles. The flowers are said to have a "naive neatness" that needs no improvement; they are narrower and smaller than the larger and flatter *I. ensata* var. *spontanea*, known as *hanashobu*.

Hanashobu is more spectacular than *kakitsubata* and has been bred intensively. It now comes in all shapes and colours, from white, through pink to deep purple, and is often cultivated in large beds in slightly ridged rows or in pots, so that they can be admired as individuals against golden folding screens.

In parts of Japan where they cannot cultivate either of these irises for lack of water, the European *I. germanica* is often grown in the same way, in large beds exclusively devoted to irises. Other irises grown are *I. tectorum* (roof iris) and the shade-loving *I. japonica*, whose wild look is perfect for the tea garden.

Flowering time summer
Size to 80cm (32in)
Conditions full sun or partial shade; slightly acid soil
Fully hardy/Z 4–9

Nelumbo nucifera
Hana-basu

By high summer the glories of the Japanese garden have long faded, and it is time for the lotus to bloom. The lotus is the flower most closely associated with Hinduism and Buddhism, and the Buddha is often portrayed in statues and images sitting on a lotus, in his state of perfect enlightenment. The lotus symbolizes the evolution of the human spirit, with its roots in the mud, its growth passing through water and air and into the sun, to open, pure and unsullied. The wheel-like formation of the petals is also said to represent the cycle of existence. The lotus is even sometimes regarded as the flower of death because Amida's Western Paradise is a lotus-filled lake, in which the dead wait to become immortal. As the young

Right, top to bottom Morning glory, *Ipomoea indica*; *Iris laevigata*; the Lotus, a sacred flower of the Buddhists.

leaves break the surface of the water they are tinged with copper, but soon turn into large scallops of blue-green foliage, remaining fresh and vibrant, even in the fierce heat of the summer sun. A succession of flowers opens over six weeks, the buds opening at dawn with an indescribable sound. The white flowers of *N. nucifera* 'Alba' have an especially powerful and sweet perfume. Lotus flowers close in the heat of the day and after a couple of days gracefully fall, one petal at a time, leaving their distinctive honeycombed seed pods. The lotus is also an important source of nourishment. The seeds, roots and leaves are all eaten, but varieties grown as food rarely flower.

The lotus is not reliably hardy, and some climates are simply not hot enough in the summer to stimulate its flowering. In these circumstances *Nymphaea* (waterlily) is a good substitute, although the flowers sit closer to the surface of the water and are not held on erect stalks, like the tall flower stems of the lotus.

Flowering time summer
Size 1.2m (4ft) above water
Conditions in full sun; in water to a depth of 60cm (24in)
Half hardy/Z 4–11

Autumn foliage

Plants that celebrate autumn with their colourful leaves were known collectively as *momichi*, but in time the term became synonymous exclusively with viewing the beautiful tones of the Japanese maple (*keade*). Even the gods, it was believed, would adorn their hair with maple leaves to pay their respect to this tree in its autumn dress.

Acer palmatum
Kaede

The Japanese maple is perhaps second only to the cherry blossom in popularity, which is why the Japanese take special holidays to view the flaming autumn tints of their maples. *Acer palmatum* is native to Japan, where it can be seen mingling on hillsides with cedars, bamboos and pines. *A. micranthum, A. tataricum* var. *ginnala* and *A. japonicum* are also native and occasionally seen in gardens, and all turn beautiful colours, but in November the temples and gardens of Kyoto are ablaze with the fiery red and orange leaves of *A. palmatum*. Although there are hundreds of fancy types of Japanese maple, some with finely cut leaves and others with variegated and purple foliage, the species *A. palmatum* is the chief focus of all the celebrations in gardens and in the wild.

Some very beautiful forms of Japanese maple have salmon-tinted foliage, which unfurls in spring, while some turn bright yellow rather than red in autumn, and others have bright red or green stems in winter. The dwarf and cut-leaf forms may be more suitable for the smaller garden, but it is better to try and avoid the purple-leafed forms, which tend to distract from carefully composed, harmonious arrangements.

Size small tree to 8m (25ft)
Pruning by cutting out over-long and crossing stems in late winter
Conditions full sun or partial shade; moist soil
Fully hardy/Z 5–8

Suitable forms of *A. palmatum*:
– 'Chitoseyama' has a hint of purple in the foliage, which turns purple-red in autumn.
– *A. p.* var. *dissectum* Dissectum Viride Group is a small, rounded shrub with deeply cut leaves and fine autumn colour.
– 'Ichigyoji' has a bold green foliage that turns bright yellow in the autumn.

Below, from left *Acer palmatum* var. *dissectum* is ideal for the smaller garden; *Acer palmatum* can be as good as any of its

– 'Katsura' has bright pink young foliage in spring, which turns flame colours in autumn.

– 'Linearilobum' has deeply cut, bright green leaves, which turn yellow in autumn.

– 'Omurayama' has finely cut green leaves, and the plant becomes elegantly pendulous with age.

– 'Osakazuki' is a rounded tree with large leaves that turn bright orange and red tints in autumn.

– 'Sango-kaku' has salmon spring tints, the leaves turn yellow in autumn and the stems are red.

Cercidiphyllum japonicum
Katsura

Thought to resemble the moon, this medium-size tree has ascending branches and beautifully rounded leaves that fire up in the autumn. As the leaves fall they give off an aroma akin to burnt, crushed sugar.
Size tree to 20m (66ft)
Pruning by removing over-long or crossing branches in late winter
Conditions sun or light shade; slightly acid soil
Fully hardy/Z 5–9

Diospyrus kaki
Kaki

The persimmon is a fine autumn tree as its yellow to orange fruits persist long after the leaves have fallen. The most edible of date plums, it is also grown for its handsome leaves, which turn yellow, orange-red and purple before they fall. In cold areas this frost-hardy plant is best grown against a wall.
Flowering time summer
Size tree to 10m (30ft)
Pruning by removing over-long or crossing branches in late winter
Conditions sheltered position in full sun; rich soil
Fully hardy/Z 4–8

Enkianthus perulatus
Dodan

A member of the same family as heathers, this large shrub has clusters of small cream- and pink-tinted bells in spring, but is more often grown for its bright red and golden-orange autumn foliage. In some gardens it is pruned so hard that it produces few flowers, although judicious pruning can enhance its habit of tiered branching. It can be grown as a hedge or mixed with evergreens as part of a tapestry hedge. A good alternative is *E. campanulatus*.
Flowering time mid-spring
Size shrub to 2m (6½ft)
Pruning by cutting out crossing or over-long shoots in early spring
Conditions sun or partial shade; moist, slightly acid soil
Fully hardy/Z 5–7

Ginkgo biloba

The leaves of the maidenhair tree turn a shade of bright butter yellow in autumn. Originally native to China, ginkgo is now found all over Japan, and can grow to an immense size.
Flowering time (catkins) spring
Size tree to 30m (100ft)
Pruning by removing diseased or dead branches in late winter or early spring
Conditions full sun; any soil
Fully hardy/Z 5–9

Nandina domestica
Nanten

Known as the sacred bamboo and native to Japan, the nanten is actually a close relative of berberis.

Above, from left *Enkianthus campanulatus*; the fruits of the persimmon, *Diospyrus kaki*; *Nandina domestica* in autumn.

In midsummer small, white flowers are carried in large, open panicles, and they are followed by red berries, which lie above the glossy, pinnate foliage. In a good autumn the leaves turn bright red, especially if the shrub has been planted in full sun, although they are tolerant of some shade. In very cold areas many of the leaves tend to fall by late winter, but it is considered to be more or less evergreen.
Flowering time midsummer
Size shrub to 2m (6ft)
Pruning by trimming back over-long shoots in mid- to late spring
Conditions full sun; moist soil
Fully hardy/Z 7–10

Other plants to consider:
– *Stewartia pseudocamellia*, each leaf of which turns a mixture of yellow, orange, green and red.
– *Styrax japonicus* and various cherries add lovely shades to the autumn garden.

Autumn flowers

The "seven grasses of autumn" have been known and used since the 11th century in Heian gardens. The selection of these seven herbaceous plants has varied over the centuries and from region to region, but in general they are the ones that flower after the summer rains and before the autumn colour comes in. Included here are some of the original seven, together with a few others that have since gained in popularity.

Left Two forms of the autumn *Anemone japonica*.

Flowering time late summer to mid-autumn
Size perennial to 1.2m (4ft)
Conditions sun or partial shade; rich, moist soil
Fully hardy/Z 5–8

Callicarpa japonica
Murasaki shikobu

Named after the author of the great 11th-century novel *The Tale of Genji*, the Japanese species *Callicarpa japonica* (beauty berry) is a low-growing, arching, deciduous shrub, which bears beautiful purple berries in autumn and winter. Its larger cousin, *C. bodinieri* var. *bondinieri* 'Profusion', is more frequently planted in Western gardens but is a much larger shrub.
Flowering time late summer
Size shrub to 1.5m (5ft)
Pruning cut back close to ground level in early spring
Conditions sun or light shade; rich soil
Fully hardy/Z 5–8

Chrysanthemum
Kiku

Extracts and essence of chrysanthemum were believed to possess miraculous powers for a longer life. Long associated with the imperial Japanese family, the plant's mythological status has made it the subject of fairy stories and legends. The large, fancy, ball-shaped flowers are not often included in formal gardens, but their presence in pots, outside temples and in domestic gardens makes them an indispensable part of the early to mid-autumn scene. Great pride is taken in the cultivation of the artificial giants, but more modest species are grown in gardens. The related *Leucanthemum* x *superbum* (formerly *Chrysanthemum* x *superbum*; shasta daisy), with simple, white, yellow-centred flowers, like a large marguerite, might flower in late autumn. These, and a number of wild asters, are suitable for the wilderness parts of the tea garden, where the bright, over-bred forms are out of place.

Anemone

Plants known as Japanese anemones have been developed from the Chinese import *Anemone hupehensis*, which has been extensively hybridized. This tall herbaceous plant with vine-like leaves is often seen in shady gardens, planted in clumps of moss and beside streams. The finest form is the single, pure white *A.* x *hybrida* 'Honorine Jobert', but there are many cultivars, with flower colours ranging from white to pale purple-pink to a deep purple-pink and some examples are double. In fertile soil it can be invasive and may need to be kept under control.

Flowering time early to late autumn

Size perennial to 1.5m (5ft)

Conditions sheltered position in full sun; rich soil

Fully hardy/Z 4–9

Eupatorium
Fujibakama

Eupatorium is known as hemp agrimony in Britain and as Joe Pye weed in the USA. The Japanese species *Eupatorium chinense* and *E. lindleyanum* are tall herbaceous plants with flattened heads of fuzzy purple or white flowers, which are adored by bees. The subdued colouring and upright habit make them excellent for semi-naturalizing.

Flowering time autumn

Size perennial 1–2m (3–6½ft)

Conditions full sun or partial shade; any moist soil

Fully hardy/Z 4–9

Below, left to right Potted chrysanthemums; the long sprays of *Lespedeza bicolor*; and the toad lily, *Tricyrtis hirta*.

Lespedeza bicolor
Hagi

The purple-flowered bush clover is a lax and arching shrub, which comes into leaf late in the season. Its purple, broom-like racemes of flowers, up to 15cm (6in) long, appear in autumn at the ends of shoots and side-shoots on wand-like stems 1–3m (3–10ft) long.

Flowering time mid- to late summer

Size shrub to 2m (6½ft)

Pruning by cutting down to ground level in early spring

Conditions full sun; well-drained soil

Fully hardy/Z 4–6

Miscanthus sinensis
Obana, susuki

Because *Miscanthus sinensis*, or fountain grass, colonizes waste ground in Japan it is rarely used as a garden plant. When it is, it is used with restraint. The silvery plumes, which appear in autumn, reach 2–4m (6–12ft) high. *M. sinensis* 'Yakushimensis Dwarf' is a low-growing form from Yakushima, the volcanic island off the south coast of Japan, which makes a rounded clump 1m (3ft) high and across. The old flower and leaf stems turn to shades of fawn, persisting into the New Year before being dispersed by the wind. Eualia grass, covering many of the hills, waves elegantly in the wind and is sometimes planted in gardens, as are various sedges (*Carex* species), often placed near streams.

Flowering time autumn

Size grass to 4m (13ft)

Conditions full sun; well-drained soil

Fully hardy/Z 5–9

Platycodon grandiflorus
Kikyo, asagao

The balloon flower, from the campanula family, has inflated and pleated flower buds that give the plant its name. The flowers, which eventually open to a wide cup, are mostly blue, but some have pink or white flowers. This compact, herbaceous plant with blue-green leaves can be grown on its own or near the edge of a stream.

Flowering time late summer

Size perennial to 60cm (24in)

Conditions sun or partial shade; moist soil

Fully hardy/Z 4–9

Tricyrtis
Hototogisu

The old Chinese name for this plant means the "oil spot plant" because its flowers are freckled with maroon to purple spots. Its Japanese name, *hototogisu*, is the same as the name for a cuckoo, which has a freckled chest. This genus, known in the West as toad lily, has only recently become popular in Japan, its wild forms with their modest and mysterious colours being suitable for planting in moist shade beside a tea garden path or near a stream.

Flowering time late summer to mid-autumn

Size perennial to 80cm (31½in)

Conditions shade; rich, moist soil

Fully hardy/Z 7

Evergreen shrubs

Japan's flora is rich in its range of native evergreen shrubs. Many are grown in and around the gardens of Kyoto. The following selection has been made for the plants' hardiness and general availability. Camellias and azaleas have already been discussed under spring-flowering shrubs (see pages 132–3), but they need to be mentioned again because they form the backbone of most evergreen schemes in Japanese gardens, especially as they can be well pruned and shaped.

Ardisia japonica
Senryo

Seen in many gardens in Kyoto and in the south, ardisias are delightful evergreen shrubs, often only hardy in sheltered spots. *Ardisia japonica* (marlberry) is a small shrub with white or pale pink flowers, which are followed by red or yellow berries. They last from autumn into winter and are used for New Year decorations. *A. crenata* (coralberry, spiceberry), which is known as *manryo*, is a larger shrub, to 2m (6½ft), with white or pink flowers followed by scarlet fruits.
Flowering time summer
Size shrub to 1m (3ft)
Pruning by removing over-long shoots in mid-spring
Conditions sheltered position in shade; moist, rich, acid soil
Half hardy/Z 4–8

Aucuba japonica
Aoki

The spotted laurels are reliable evergreen shrubs with glossy foliage. They love shade and tolerate the dry soil among the roots of large trees. In autumn female shrubs bear small clusters of large red berries, so they are sometimes called Japanese hollies. There are forms with yellow-spotted leaves and others with orange or yellow berries, but in Japanese gardens the most popular plant is the species or its narrow-leafed form, "Salicifolia".
Flowering time mid-spring
Size shrub to 3m (10ft)
Pruning by removing crossing or over-long shoots in late winter or early spring
Conditions shade or partial shade; any soil
Fully hardy/Z 7–10

Daphne odora
Jinchoge

This small evergreen shrub carries its deliciously sweet-scented, pink-white flowers in late winter to early spring. Most often seen in gardens in the form "Aureomarginata", which has gold-edged leaves. A lovely plant to tuck unobtrusively in a mixed planting.
Flowering time late winter to early spring
Size shrub to 1.5m (5ft)
Pruning by removing over-long shoots after flowering
Conditions sun or partial shade; rich, moist, slightly acid soil
Fully hardy/8–10

Elaeagnus x ebbingei

There are several species of elaeagnus, including *Elaeagnus pungens*, *E. glabra* and *E. macrophylla*, but the most common green-leaved form is the hybrid *E.* x *ebbingei*, with dusty green leaves, which are silvery beneath. In autumn small, creamy white, bell-shaped flowers are born in the leaf axils, almost out of sight, but their scent can carry far. This is a wonderful evergreen for mixed hedges, when it can be pruned to maintain a neat shape, screens and as a general evergreen backdrop. Variegated forms are offered by nurseries, but are not appropriate for a Japanese garden. The growth of *E.* x *ebbingei* can be a bit rangy and will need some tidying.
Flowering time autumn
Size shrub to 4m (13ft)
Pruning by cutting back over-long shoots in mid-spring
Conditions full sun or partial shade; any soil
Fully hardy/Z 7–9

Fatsia japonica

Native to the forests of Japan, the Japanese aralia has large, distinctive, glossy, ivy-like leaves. The flowers, which resemble those of ivy, are like small explosions; they are initially pale cream-green but turn almost black. A hybrid between *Fatsia* and *Hedera* (ivy), *Fatshedera lizei* (tree ivy) is a rather sprawling but smaller plant, to about 2m (6½ft).
Flowering time autumn
Size shrub to 4m (12ft)
Pruning not needed
Conditions sheltered position in full sun or partial shade; any soil
Fully hardy/Z 7–9

Mahonia japonica

An erect, pinnate, holly-like plant related to the berberis, this mahonia has yellow flower spikes in winter and early spring. All have sweetly scented flowers and a strong, architectural shape. When too woody and overgrown, prune hard, removing the old stems first, immediately after flowering.
Flowering time late autumn to early spring
Size shrub to 2m (6½ft)
Pruning by cutting back over-long shoots after flowering

Conditions sheltered position in partial shade; any reasonable soil
Fully hardy/Z 6–8

Osmanthus fragrans
Kinmokusei

A popular shrub in Japan, the fragrant olive or sweet tea is famed for its creamy autumn flowers, but it is not very hardy. A hardier hybrid, *O. fortunei*, is more suitable for most gardens, or you could try *O. heterophyllus*, known as *hi-ragi*, a broad, holly-leaved shrub.
Flowering time autumn
Size shrub to 6m (20ft)
Pruning by cutting back to maintain shape in mid-spring
Conditions sheltered position in sun or partial shade; any reasonable soil
Fully hardy/Z 8–9

Photinia glabra
Kaname-mochi

Photinias are mostly handsome, broad-leafed evergreen trees and shrubs, often planted to create a backdrop or shade. White flowers are carried in loose panicles from spring to summer, followed by the rosy red flush of young foliage, especially evident in hybrids such

as 'Red Robin' and 'Birmingham'. Photinias are pretty hardy and can be kept at a manageable height through pruning. They can also be grown as a hedge.
Flowering time late spring to early summer
Size shrub to 5m (15ft)
Pruning by cutting out crossing and badly positioned stems in early spring
Conditions full sun or partial shade; any moist soil
Fully hardy/Z 7–8

Pieris japonica
A-sebi

The Japanese name, *a-sebi*, literally means "horse-drunk", for its poisonous effects on browsing animals. This compact shrub is a reasonably hardy evergreen, with pendulous clusters of white, lily-of-the-valley flowers in early spring. The young growth is tinted pink. (The Chinese species *P. formosa* has brilliant red-bronze young growth but is not as hardy. The American species, *P. floribunda*, is hardy.) Pieris prefers acid soil and plenty of humus but can withstand quite dry conditions in late summer. It is often grown in a container. More commonly seen as a large shrub, it can grow into a small tree.

Opposite and above, left to right
The yellow-berried *Ardisia japonica*; *Fatsia japonica* flower buds; young foliage of *Photinia* 'Red Robin'; scented spikes of *Mahonia japonica*; heather-like flowers of *Pieris japonica*; and *Osmanthus heterophyllus* flowers.

There are a number of small-leaved and dwarf forms, including 'Green Heath', which grows to 60cm (24in).
Flowering time late winter to spring
Size shrub to 3m (10ft)
Pruning by removing dead shoots after flowering
Conditions full sun or light shade; acid soil

Topiary and hedges

Mixed groups of camellias, azaleas, pieris and photinias, evergreen oaks and hollies are often clipped into *o-karikomi*, the Japanese equivalent of Western topiary, and hedges. Low hedges of *Camellia sinensis* (tea plant) are often planted near tea gardens; tea plants have much smaller leaves and flowers than the more ornamental camellias and are less hardy.

Evergreen trees and conifers

The general Japanese name for conifers is *shohaku-rui*, and they were said – especially the tall, straight pines – to draw the gods down to Earth, while the Shintoists beat wooden planks to attract them. Such evergreen trees have been regarded as symbols of chastity, consistency and loyalty.

Chamaecyparis obtusa
Hinoki

Often planted in forests with the Japanese cedar, the Hinoki cypress is a valuable timber tree. It is more commonly seen in gardens in its dwarf forms: *C. obtusa* 'Nana Gracilis' grows to 3m (10ft) high and *C. obtusa* 'Pygmaea' reaches 1.5m (5ft) high. These smaller versions have more character than most cypress-like trees, with their twisted whorls of vivid young growth. Exceptionally hardy, all three plants can tolerate exposed situations. They can also be successfully clipped into hedges and topiary-style (*o-karikomi*) shapes.

Size tree to 20m (66ft)

Pruning not needed but remove dead or diseased branches

Conditions full sun; slightly acid soil

Fully hardy/Z 4–8

Cryptomeria japonica
Sugi

After the pine, the most important and sacred conifer is the Japanese cedar (*Cryptomeria japonica*). This is capable of living for more than 2,000 years and is often planted as a sign of virtue and as a guardian to Buddhist and Shinto shrines.

Cryptomerias are planted in most of the commercial forests in Japan. It is an easily worked timber and is used extensively in the building industry. Its aroma makes the wood prized for sake casks. The cryptomeria is a towering, conical tree, with finely dissected, scaly foliage. It is often coppiced in gardens, and the new growth is pruned into tiers with shaped, pompom-like foliage at the ends. It can also be planted on its own or as part of a mixed hedge. There are many cultivated varieties of *C. japonica*, but most are merely curiosities.

Size tree to 25m (82ft)

Pruning not needed

Conditions full sun or partial shade; deep, moist, slightly acid soil

Fully hardy/Z 6–9

Other conifers and evergreen trees for the Japanese garden:

– *Chamaecyparis pisifera* (Sawara cypress) is a conical tree to 20m (66ft); 'Filifera' has dark green, thread-like foliage; 'Squarrosa' has soft sprays of dark green foliage.

– *Juniperus chinensis* (Chinese juniper), known as *ibuki*, this tree has bright green, angular growth to 20m (66ft).

– *Podocarpus macrophyllus* (*kusamaki*), known as *maki*, this conical tree grows to 15m (50ft).

– *Sciadopitys verticillata* (Japanese umbrella pine) is a conical tree, known as *koya maki*, with leathery, spoke-like needles and growing to 20m (66ft).

– *Taxus cuspidata* (Japanese yew) is an upright shrub or small tree, known as *ichi*, growing to 15m (50ft).

– *Thujopsis dolobrata* (hiba, false arborvitae), known as *asunaro*, is a dense, conical tree growing to 20m (66ft).

Far left *Thujopsis dolobrata*.
Left *Podocarpus macrophyllus*.

Above, from left Japanese red pine, *Pinus densiflora*; Japanese black pine, *Pinus thunbergii*; Japanese white pine, *Pinus parviflora*.

Pinus densiflora
Aka–matsu

A fine tree with pinkish-red bark and a rounded head, the Japanese red pine is often pruned to accentuate its soft crown and show its elegant, branched structure. *P. densiflora*, or 'Umbraculifera', known as *tanyosho*, is a compact, rounded or flat-topped bushy tree, reaching 2–3m (6½–10ft). This dwarf pine can be planted in groves over small hills, giving the impression that it is within a larger landscape.
Size tree to 20m (66ft)
Pruning needs little pruning to develop a strong structure
Conditions full sun; any well-drained soil
Fully hardy/Z 3–7

Pinus parviflora
Go-yo-matsu

Native to Japan, the Japanese white pine has shorter, grey-green needles and is slower growing and more manageable than either *P. densiflora* or *P. thunbergii*, but it will eventually make a large, multi-stemmed, mounding tree. There

are many dwarf forms, including 'Glauca Nana' and 'Hagaromo Seedling suitable for small gardens.
Size tree to 20m (66ft)
Pruning needs little pruning to develop a strong structure
Conditions full sun; any well-drained soil
Fully hardy/Z 4–7

Pinus thunbergii
Kuro-matsu

More rugged and darker in leaf and bark than *P. densiflora*, the Japanese black pine is generally pruned into more horizontal and dramatic windswept postures. It is the most popular pine for bonsai.
Size tree to 25m (82ft)
Pruning during the early growing season
Conditions full sun; any well-drained soil
Fully hardy/Z 6–8

Other pines suitable for Japanese-style gardens:
Pinus sylvestris (Scots pine), especially *P. sylvestris* 'Watereri'; *P. mugo* (dwarf mountain pine) grows to 3.5m (11ft) high and is suitable for very small gardens.

Right *Cryptomeria japonica*.

Sacred pines
Pines (or *matsu*, in Japanese, which means "waiting for a god") were regarded as the king of trees and were an important poetic image. The pine boughs are often draped with decorations at New Year, for the moon-viewing celebrations and at weddings. One of the most important natural Japanese landscapes is Matsushima Bay, in northern Honshu, which is dotted with more than 800 pine-clad islands.

There are few Japanese gardens that do not possess a pine tree. Together with azaleas and maples, they are one of the fundamental ingredients. Many hours of loving care are spent plucking their needles and pruning their boughs, creating shapes that deliberately evoke trees bent by the winds on mountains and seashores.

The two most popular pines in Japanese gardens are *Pinus densiflora* (red pine) and *P. thunbergii* (black pine), regarded as the female and male pine.

Miscellaneous plants

This selection includes plants that can be randomly placed beside the tea path or grown in shady courtyards. Many of them have hundreds of interesting, even quirky, variations, and they are often specially grown in pots so that they can be highlighted. They are not usually grown for planting out in the garden, where they might disrupt the overall scheme. Some of the epiphytic ferns have become the subject of plant breeders' obsessions and are grown in pots as show plants. The selection also includes some recommendations for suitable bamboos and palms.

Alcea rosea
Tachia-oi

It's quite a surprise to find that the hollyhock is not an old European cottage-garden plant but one that originated in China, where it has been cultivated for over a thousand years. It has been popular in Japan since Heian times and is still very popular, especially in gardens of small houses and those in side streets, where its tall, narrow growth is ideal and dramatic.
Flowering time early to midsummer
Size perennial to 2.4m (8ft)
Conditions full sun; any soil
Fully hardy/Z 6–9

Equisetum hyemale
Tokusa

The small tufted mare's tail of Western gardens is a pernicious but attractive weed that likes wet soils. Japanese forms are less invasive and rather more stately. The evergreen, vertical, leafless stems of *E. hyemale* (Dutch rush, rough horsetail) are an arresting sight. Also grown as a pot plant.
Size perennial to 1.5m (5ft)
Conditions sun or partial shade; moist soil
Fully hardy/Z 4–9

Farfugium japonicum
Tsuwa-buki

The yellow flowers of this evergreen perennial with scalloped leaves are similar to ligularias. Many variegated forms have been developed, the most common being 'Aureomaculatum', which has random yellow spots on the leaves. The yellow flowers brighten up damp, shady spots.
Flowering time autumn to early winter
Size perennial to 60cm (24in)
Conditions partial shade; moist soil
Fully hardy/Z 7–9

Far left The hollyhock, *Alcea rosea*. **Left** Leaf stems of *Equisetum hyemale*.

Hosta
Giboshi

Hostas, or plantain lilies, have been planted in Japanese gardens since Heian times, primarily for their handsome foliage, less so for their flowers. *Hosta sieboldiana*, one of the hostas with the largest leaves, can be seen growing at 1,000m (3,280ft) at the foot of Mount Fuji. *H. plantaginea*, which is native to China, has white, scented flowers, while *H. montana* and *H. tardiva*, both native to Japan, are grown for their handsome foliage. *H. ventricosa*, which was also introduced from China, is particularly striking with beautiful violet flowers and strong, green-ribbed foliage.

Hostas, like so many other plants in Japan, were selected for their variety of leaf forms during the 19th century. Plants with variegated and twisted leaves were usually grown as specimens for display, rather than as part of the garden scheme. Incidentally, some gourmets, other than slugs, consider the blanched stems of *H. sieboldiana* a delicacy. After covering the stems with straw to blanch them, the long, spear-like shoots grow to several centimetres and are then steamed and eaten.
Flowering time summer
Size perennial 25–90cm (10–36in)
Conditions a sheltered position in sun or partial shade; moist soil
Fully hardy/Z 4–9

Houttuynia cordata
Dokudami

Houttuynia is grown in many Japanese gardens, especially near water, but it can be very invasive. The heart-shaped leaves have a strong odour when crushed, while the small white flowers are picked to make herbal tea. There are a number of variegated forms, but the plain green kind is the most popular.
Flowering time spring
Size perennial to 30cm (12in)
Conditions full sun; moist soil
Fully hardy/Z 5–9

Lilium
Yuri

Lilium auratum, known as *yama-yuri*, is the golden-rayed lily of Japan, and it caused a sensation when it was introduced to Britain in 1862. It has large, white, trumpet-like flowers with freckles and golden streaks inside. It is one of the few scented plants native to Japan, where it may be found growing in the volcanic ash of extinct volcanoes. It is a fussy plant that needs acid soil with plenty of humus. Hybrids between *L. auratum* and *L. speciosum* are much easier to grow. In Japanese gardens lilies are grown in pots and put out on seasonal display.

The unscented but vibrant *L. lancifolium* (tiger lily), with its orange and yellow, heavily spotted, reflexed flowers, has

Right, top to bottom *Farfugium japonicum* is evergreen; an oriental lily hybrid 'Royal Class'; the boldest of hosta leaves, *Hosta sieboldiana*.

been grown extensively as a food (where the bulbs are eaten) and is only rarely allowed to flower.
Flowering time late summer to early autumn
Size bulb to 1.5m (5ft)
Conditions full sun; acid soil
Fully hardy/Z 4–9

Ophiopogon japonicus
Ja-no-hige, Ryo-no-hige

Japanese mondo grass is a thick, leathery, grass-like plant, which can be vigorous enough to colonize whole gardens and needs only a little maintenance in its early days to get established. Related to the larger Liriope (lilyturf), it has dark green leaves, which curve over. Carpets of it can set off larger plants, such as groups of acers, azaleas and bamboos. The flowers are white or pale blue and followed by small black berries, but both are fairly insignificant. The dwarf, tufted *O. japonicus* 'Minor' is a better bet in small gardens. The black-leaved lilyturf, *O. planiscapus* 'Nigrescens', which gets to 20cm (8in), is popular in Western gardens and is often used in contemporary designs.
Flowering time summer
Size perennial to 60cm (24in)
Conditions full sun or partial shade; slightly acid soil
Fully hardy/Z 6–10

Pachysandra terminalis
Fukiso

This evergreen has been planted extensively in Western gardens as excellent groundcover in fairly dry shade, and it forms a perfect carpet of serrated leaves. In some parts of the world it has been used so much as groundcover that it has become ubiquitous, but this shouldn't detract from a handsome plant. The small white flowers are quite attractive but are not worth growing for their own sake. The variegated form, 'Variegata', is less vigorous than the species.

Flowering time early summer
Size perennial to 20cm (8in)
Conditions shade; any soil
Fully hardy/Z 4–8

Left, top to bottom *Phyllostachys nigra* 'Boryana', or black bamboo; *Shibataea kumasasa*; *Pseudosasa japonica*, or arrow bamboo.

Bamboos
Taki

Although most Japanese gardens are cultivated in temperate climates, where plants like azaleas, cherries and plums grow well, in more tropical or subtropical climates it may be possible to grow only those plants that are better suited to the heat. Even in temperate climates, however, you can try the "tropical look" with plants that are quite hardy. Bamboos can be highly invasive plants so site carefully. The bamboos listed below like full sun or partial shade and rich soil, unless stated otherwise.
– *Phyllostachys aurea*, the fishpole bamboo or golden bamboo, which grows to 10m (33ft), has mid-green canes, which age to golden-brown. It will spread, so contain the roots. The shorter *P. aureosulcata* (yellow-groove bamboo), which grows to 6m (20ft) high, has

Above The dwarf form of *Ophiopogon japonica*.

brown-green canes, attractively ribbed with yellow.
– *Phyllostachys edulis*, the evergreen moso bamboo, has become naturalized in the woods around Japanese towns where it is often harvested for its huge stems. It can grow to 6m (20ft) or more. In colder climates it will not reach these dimensions, which are seen in the southern half of Japan. *P. edulis* 'Heterocycla' has fascinating tortoiseshell-shaped internodes. The hardy *P. vivax*, which makes a good alternative, has grey canes and can get to 25m (82ft).
– *Phyllostachys nigra*, the dramatic black bamboo, is equally popular in Japan and in the West for its polished black stems, especially in the form 'Munro'. The distinctive canes become black with age and are a dramatic contrast to the

abundant green leaves. It can grow to 5m (16ft).

– *Pleioblastus humilis* is a fairly low-growing bamboo, growing to 1.5m (5ft), with dark green canes and light green leaves and preferring a sheltered position in full sun or partial shade. It can be invasive, so contain the roots. The much smaller *P. pygmaeus* (pygmy bamboo), growing to 40cm (16in), can be planted as groundcover and clipped down to 5–10cm (2–4in) high, being a substitute for lawns or moss

– *Pseudosasa japonica*, formerly known as *Sasa japonica*, is a tough and rather invasive bamboo with dark green leaves on pale beige stems. It can grow to 6m (20ft).

– *Shibataea kumasasa* is a useful bamboo that can be allowed to grow naturally, to about 1.5m (5ft), or clipped into a low hedge, about 60cm (24in) high. It prefers a rich, moist soil.

Ferns

Japanese ferns are regarded as excellent, shapely plants for softening the hard edges of groups of rocks and for being a sympathetic foil to the glossy evergreens, which are required to give the wooded, wilderness effect to the path in tea gardens. The sensitive fern, *Onoclea sensibilis*, and the royal fern, *Osmunda regalis*, are both suitable for the Japanese garden. Camellias, with light (not bright) colours and simple flowers, aucubas, nandinas and acers combine well with ferns.

Palms

As long as they are grown in sheltered positions, many palms are surprisingly hardy. Although Japanese gardens tend to be associated more with temperate flora, it is not inappropriate to use

palms and other exotic plants, providing that the same design principles are followed.

– *Cycas revoluta*, the sago palm, is an ancient plant that is native to the southern islands of Japan. It is a beautiful, popular, glossy evergreen, which looks like a cross between a palm and a fern. It can grow to 2m (6½ft) and requires full sun and moist, rich soil. It is, however, only marginally hardy, and is rarely seen in gardens north of Kyoto. Even in Kyoto the sago palm has to be wrapped up in winter, and, just like everything else in Japanese gardens, this elaborate wrapping has been raised to the level of an art form.

– *Rhapis excelsa* (Shuro), the miniature fan palm, which was previously known as *Chamaerops excelsa*, is native to China and was introduced to Japan in the 19th century. Stockier and spinier than the Chusan palm,

Above *Trachycarpus fortunei*, the Chusan palm, is hardy.

but not quite as hardy, it is still a valuable addition to the tropical look in a temperate garden, growing to 5m (16ft). It requires a sheltered position in light shade and any soil.

– *Trachycarpus fortunei* (*To-juro*), the frost-hardy Chusan palm, was originally grown for its yield of fibre, and it has since become naturalized in many parts of the country. It grows quite erect, to 20m (66ft), and the fan-shaped leaves are 1m (3ft) long and 75cm (30in) wide. Protect from cold winds and keep them in a sheltered position in full sun or light shade and any soil.

Far left The sensitive fern, *Onoclea sensibilis*. **Left** *Osmunda regalis*, the royal fern.

General care and maintenance

There is a curious ambiguity about the Japanese garden. On the one hand, maintaining a spread of gravel, a rock or two, a pine tree and bamboo should require very little work. On the other hand, a dynamic Japanese garden, carpeted with moss and planted with several trees and shrubs around a pond, can in fact involve a high level of maintenance.

Meticulous care and scrupulous cleanliness are required in the maintenance of even the more naturalistic tea gardens. The Japanese gardener, as in so many of the Japanese arts, is careful to pay inordinate attention to every detail. All in all, despite the Japanese garden's more minimal design, its upkeep – with detailed pruning, brushing, raking, weeding and tending – easily provides as much maintenance work as is required in any traditional Western garden.

Pruning

In Japan, teams of professionals descend on public and private gardens once or twice a year in order to carry out the specialized job of pruning. If pruning is done only once a year, most shrubs and trees can be tackled from early to late autumn, but some plants, such as plums, require pruning immediately after flowering. While electrical shears are disapproved of by professionals, they are in fact the most efficient method for large gardens and hedges, although camellias and large-leafed plants are better pruned with a pair of secateurs (pruners) so that the foliage is not shredded and ruined. Furthermore, pruning is not simply about creating a specific shape, but frequently about recognizing and then highlighting a plant's natural shape and structure. It can take many years of experience to prune as successfully as a professional gardener.

Above left Sweeping leaves in autumn.
Above right Renewing a fence.

Pruning is particularly important because Japanese gardens are often quite densely planted, and you need to decide how much light should be allowed to fall on the ground between shrubs to encourage the growth of moss, mondo grass or other groundcover plants. Too much light and some plants will burn in the sun, while too much shade might stunt or kill plants, leaving the earth exposed, dusty and brown. The art is to allow just the right amount of light to fall to create attractive, dappled shade and a green surface.

Weeding

Although Japanese gardens do not have flower borders, all their plants, carpets of moss and paths will need regular weeding. Weed-suppressing matting and the use of weed killers could be used, but, however you proceed, note that Japanese gardening is meant to be meditative and calming, and should be approached with gentility, patience and attentiveness.

Raking gravel

One of the most meditative practices is raking gravel in a dry garden (*kare sansui*). In Temple gardens the rhythmic, focused motions of raking are still part of the spiritual practices of Zen monks and their acolytes. Though the sharp grit is coarse enough to resist heavy downpours of rain, after a few days or a week it will need raking again.

In the famous garden of Shisendo, in Kyoto, the surface of the dry garden is covered by light sand, which requires brushing rather than raking. Bamboo and brushwood besoms are used to sweep the sand into patterns. These brooms are also used to

Right Elaborate frames are used to extend the weeping boughs of cherries.
Bottom right The bandaging of an old pine in hessian.

sweep debris and leaves off paths, and to make sure that the autumn leaves do not lie on the moss for too long. Finally, check that the tea path, made of stepping stones, is kept clean and free of moss and slimy algae.

Other tasks

Other occasional maintenance work might involve the repair and rebinding of bamboo fences and gates. Tree supports are elaborate constructs, with black and natural-coloured jute and sisal being used to bind branches to their supports (synthetic black "jute" is available and lasts considerably longer).

Some larger Japanese gardens have lawns, but the grass is coarse and cannot be mowed too closely. Where spreading dwarf bamboos are used instead of grass, they will need shearing once or twice a year to keep them down to 10cm (4in) at most.

Unless you have a natural stream or spring, water gardens will need a certain amount of upkeep. Pump filters must be cleaned and pools dredged to prevent them from silting up and to keep the water clean and fresh for any koi or common carp that you may wish to keep.

Glossary

Amida Buddha The form of the Buddha whose promise of a Western Paradise influenced garden makers in the Heian period.

Aminoshidate A long pine-clad peninsula on the north coast of Honshu, a famous scenic spot in Japan often symbolically reproduced in gardens.

Aware An emotional attitude to the natural world that infected the sensibility of Heian courtiers.

Bakufu The military bureaucracies that acted for the emperor.

Carp stone Appearing at a waterfall base, as if on the point of leaping. Indicates the strivings of man.

Cha-niwa Tea garden.

Cha-noyu The tea ceremony.

Chonin The merchant class, especially those who enjoyed a period of wealth during the Edo period.

Chozubachi Taller style of water basin, often placed where it can be reached from verandahs.

Confucius (d. 479BC) Chinese sage who laid down moral principles, especially popular during the Edo period when Buddhism waned.

Crane Island Part of the Mystic Isle myth. Cranes carried the immortals on their backs and became symbols of longevity.

Daimyo A lord who owned land.

Dyana Meaning meditation, this Sanskrit word is at the root of the word Zen.

Edo (1603–1867) The period when the Tokugawa shogunate ruled Japan from its new capital in Edo, now modern-day Tokyo.

Eisai This Buddhist monk was attributed with bringing both Zen and the first successfully transplanted tea plants to Japan in the 13th century.

Enshu, Kabori Early 17th-century garden designer and town planner whose mixed taste set new standards for garden design.

Fuji-san Mount Fuji, the sacred mountain sometimes reproduced symbolically in gardens.

Fuzei Taste.

Genji, Tales of Highly influential novel of the Heian period, written by Murasaki Shikobu.

Geomancy Chinese system of beliefs on how buildings, cities and gardens should be laid out relative to the directions, colours and elements. Includes the principles of yin-yang and Feng-shui.

Go-shintai Shinto term for an area that is considered to be the abode of the Gods.

Heian (AD785–1184) The period during which a new capital was created in Kyoto until the shogunate moved to Kamakura.

Hiei-san Mountain overlooking Kyoto, views of which were coveted by garden designers who wanted to borrow its form; *see also* Shakkei.

Hojo The abbot's quarters of Zen temples where most dry Zen gardens were laid out.

Horai The central island in the ancient Chinese myth of the Mystic Isles, often portrayed by a large upright rock.

Left A straight path with randomly set stones, leading to the temple of Jiko-in, Nara.

Immortals Inhabitants of the Mystic Isles who possessed the secret of the elixir of eternal youth. Mystic Isles were constructed in ponds in the hope of luring them to earth.

Ishe-tate-so These monks of the 14th and 15th centuries, called "rock-setting monks", designed the first *kare-sansui* or dry gardens.

Iwa-kura Literally "boulder-seat". Shintoists believed rocks possessed spirits, and certain rocks were given the status of gods.

Kamakura (1185–1392) A period when the shogunate moved its headquarters from Kyoto to Kamakura, south of modern-day Tokyo.

Kame-shima Island in the shape of a turtle.

Kami The Shinto term for gods.

Kare-sansui The dry landscape garden where water is substituted by sand and gravel.

Kawara-mono The lowest caste attributed with having helped to build *kare-sansui* dry gardens during the Muromachi period.

Koan Zen riddle used to achieve a state of emptiness of mind, and a trigger for enlightenment.

Kyoto The most important capital in the history of Japan for garden-making.

Machiya Smaller merchant town houses that framed small *tsubo-niwa,* or courtyard gardens.

Mappo The Buddhist Age of Ending Law, starting in the 11th century, was the last of three ages predicted by the Buddha, inducing pessimism.

Matsushima Pine-clad islands off the north-east coast of Japan; they are so striking that they have inspired their reproduction in many gardens.

Meiji restoration (1868) The restoration of the emperor as acting head of state, his move to Tokyo and the end of the shogunate rule.

Mitate Recycled building materials, such as millstones, incorporated into garden paths and buildings, showing their owners' refined taste.

Momoyama (1568–1603) The era of the generals, especially Totomi Hideyoshi, who unified Japan. The last general was Ieyasu Tokugawa, whose family ruled throughout the Edo period.

Mu Nothingness, an aspect of Zen that reveals itself in the empty spaces of sand in some dry Zen gardens.

Muromachi (1393–1568) The shogunate returned from Kamakura to Kyoto; possibly the most intensely creative period in Japanese history, which saw both the dry *kare-sansui* gardens and tea gardens come of age.

Mystic Isles *See* Horai, Crane Island and Turtle Islands.

Naka-kuguri Literally "middle crawl through gate" or stooping gate, a gate that deliberately induced a sense of humility before entering the tea house.

Nara (AD 712–94) Nara was the last of the ancient capitals, 50 miles south of Kyoto, before a new capital was built in Kyoto.

Nigiriguchi A small hatch-like entrance to the tea house, whereby the guest entered on his hands and knees.

No-da-te A more informal tea ceremony conducted outdoors.

O-karikomi The japanese form of topiary in which plants are clipped into abstract shapes.

Pagoda A Japanese and Chinese building that contained relics and treasures of the Buddha or his followers. These were often symbolically carved in stone and placed in gardens.

Peng-lai The original name for Mount Horai (*see also* Horai).

Pure Land Paradise The Buddha's abode for the afterlife, thought to be in the West. Ponds were built, especially in the Heian and Kamakura periods, to evoke this paradise.

Rikyu Japan's most famous tea-master, whose influence on the nature of the tea ceremony and garden is still felt today.

Roji Literally dewy ground or dewy path, the tea path that leads to the tea house.

Right A superb example of Japanese-style topiary or *o-karikomi*, using clipped azaleas, designed by the great Kabori Enshu at Raikyu-ji, Takahashi.

Roji-mon Entrance gate to the tea garden or *roji*.

Ryoan-ji The most famous of the dry Zen gardens in Kyoto, believed to have been built in 1499.

Sakuteiki The first and highly influential garden treatise, written in the 10th century.

Samurai A soldier in service of a lord (*daimyo*).

Sanzon Stone arrangements of the Buddhist Trinity.

Sesshu During the 15th century Sesshu was an influential Japanese brush and ink painter who was also a gardener and Zen monk.

Shakkei Literally "borrowed landscape", the drawing of distant views to become part of the garden scene.

Shibumi Derived from the word meaning astringent, this is the minimalist, unpretentious worldly aesthetic of the Edo period that replaced the earlier and more spiritual term *wabi-sabi*.

Shigemori, Mirei The most influential Japanese garden designer of the 20th century.

Shiki-no-himorogi Sacred dwelling place for a deity.

Shime The binding of artefacts, rocks and trees as part of the Shinto religion. The word *shima*, or garden, may have derived from this source.

Shin gyo and so An expression to suggest the mixture of the formal, the informal and the intermediate that described different social and physical patterns, such as paving.

Shinden Literally meaning "sleeping hall", this is the main residence at the centre of the Pond Gardens of the Heian period.

Shinto The native animistic religion of Japan.

Shishi-odoshi The deer scarer, a bamboo device that when filled with water tips and smacks against a rock.

Shogun Military leader.

Shoin architecture An architecture style developed in the Muromachi period.

Soan The rustic style of tea-house architecture.

Sode-gaki Sleeve fences, small sections of bamboo and rush fences that divide up views of the garden from the house.

Sumeru A Hindu mountain (Meru) that to the Japanese Buddhist became Mount Shumisen.

Tatami Woven rush matting that was especially favoured for the floors of Japanese tea houses.

Tokonoma The alcove in a tea house.

Tsubo-niwa Courtyard garden.

Tsukubai A low crouching basin found en route to the tea house, usually with a lantern.

Tsuru-shima A vertical rock used in Japanese gardens to represent a crane island.

Turtle Island Derived from the Mystic Isles myths, which were said to float on the backs of turtles. Turtle islands are abstract rock arrangements where flippers and heads may be discernible.

Wabi-Sabi Meaning "withered loneliness", this term also describes parts of the tea ceremony.

Yatsuhashi An eight-plank zigzag bridge that crosses over streams and ponds, often planted with irises.

Yugen Suggests a mystery that goes beyond what can be seen.

Zen Buddhism A form of Buddhism introduced to Japan from China in the 13th century. Zen heavily influenced the arts, especially gardens such as the *kare-sansui* and tea garden.

Useful addresses

United Kingdom

UK Bamboo Supplies Limited
Unit 18, Donkin Road
Armstrong Industrial Estate
Washington
Tyne and Wear NE37 1PF
Tel 0191 417 2915
sales@ukbamboosupplies.com
www.ukbamboosupplies.com

Glendoick Gardens Ltd
Glendoick, Glencarse
Perth and Kinross
Perth PH2 7NS
Scotland
Tel 01738 860205
Rhododendrons and azaleas

Heron's Bonsai
Wiremill Lane
Newchapel
Nr Lingfield
Surrey RH7 6HJ
Tel 01342 832657
www.herons.co.uk
*Japanese garden design and
bonsai specialists*

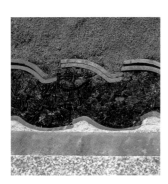

Japan Garden Co.
15 Bank Crescent, Ledbury
Herefordshire HR8 1AA
Tel 01531 630091
sales@japangarden.co.uk
Japangarden.co.uk
Lanterns, screens, fences

Japanese Garden Supplies
Millstone, Mill Lane
Worthing
West Sussex BN13 3DF (office only)
Tel 01903 691167
info@japanesegardensupplies.co.uk
Japanese garden supplies

Jungle Giants
Ferney Hall
Onibury, Craven Arms
Shropshire SY7 9BJ
Tel 01584 856200
www.junglegiants.co.uk
Bamboo plants and materials

Junker's Nursery Ltd
PMA Plant Specialists
Lower Mead, West Hatch
Taunton, Somerset TA3 5RN
Tel 01823 480774
www.junker.net
*Japanese maples, dogwoods and
wisteria*

Kenchester Water Gardens
Church Road, Lyde, Hereford
Herefordshire HR1 3AB
Tel 01432 270981
Water products, waterlilies and irises

Rhino Rock Landscapes
Addlestone Road
East Peckham, Tonbridge
Kent KN12 5DP
Tel 01622 872403
www.buildajapanesegarden.com
Plants, fences, buildings, lanterns

Rockfeatures
Wilton Farm
Marlow Road, Little Marlow
Buckinghamshire SL7 3RR
Tel 01628 533335
www.rockfeatures.co.uk
*Fibreglass and cement
imitation rocks*

Silverland Stone
Holloway Hill, Chertsey
Surrey KT16 OAE
Tel 01932 570094
www.silverlandstone.co.uk
Rocks

Thornhayes Nursery
St Andrews Wood, Dulford,
Cullompton, Devon EX15 2DF
Tel 01884 266746
Wide range of trees

United States

Bamboo Gardens of Washington
5035 – 196th Ave NE
Redmond, WA 98074
Tel (425) 868-5166
bamboogardens@earthlink.net
*Bamboos, poles, fences, granite
lanterns and basins*

Bamboo and Koi Garden
2115 SW Borland Road
West Linn, OR 97068
Tel (503) 638-0888
bambookoigarden@aol.com
Various supplies

Cherry Blossom Gardens
www.cherryblossomgardens.com
Tel (952) 758-1923
Japanese garden ornaments

Jade Mountain Bamboo Nursery
5020 116th St. E. (off Canyon Road)
Tacoma, WA 98446
Tel (253) 548-1129
www.jademountainbamboo.com
Bamboo and garden accessories

Japanese Garden
PO Box 3847
Portland, OR 97208
Tel (503) 223-1321
www.japanesegarden.com
Bells, lanterns, bonsai and ikebana

The Japanese Garden Database
1911 Brandywine Street
Philadelphia, PA 19130
www.jgarden.org
Search engine for suppliers

Japanese Garden Fences Inc.
P.O. Box 2212
Pawcatuck CT 06379
Tel (860) 599-2348
info@japanesegardenfences.com
Handcrafted sode-gake fences

Tatami Room
466 20th Street
Oakland, CA 94612
Tatamiroom@yahoo.com
*Bamboo blinds, tatami matting,
lanterns and water basins*

Australia

Garden Grove
1150 Golden Grove Road
Golden Grove, Adelaide SA 5125
Tel 8 8251 1111
www.gardengrove.com
Nursery and garden supplies centre

Universal Rocks
20 Hearne Street, Mortdale
NSW 2223
Tel 2 9533 7400
www.universalrocks.com.au
Artificial rocks and landscapes

Canada

The Angelgrove Tree Seed Co.
P.O. Box 74, 141 Hart Path Road
Riverhead, Harbour Grace NL
A0A 3P0
www.angelgroveseeds.com
Tree seeds for Japanese trees

Burns Water Gardens
Baltimore, Ontario OKOK 1 CO
Tel (905) 372-2737
Waterlilies, aquatic plants, ponds

Societies and Journals

Japan Garden Society
www.jgs.org.uk

Journal of Japanese Gardening
www.rotheien.com

Gardens to Visit

www.jgarden.org/gardens offers a
worldwide listing of gardens.

United Kingdom
Holland Park Gardens, London
(Tel 020 7471 9813)
Kew Gardens, London (Tel 020
8332 5655; www.rbgkew.org.uk)
Pine Lodge, Cornwall (Tel 01726
735000; www.pine-lodge.co.uk)
Tatton Park, Cheshire (Tel 01625
534400; www.tattonpark.org.uk)
Australia
Cowra Japanese Gardens, Cowra,
NSW (Tel 2 6341 2233)
Edogawa Commemorative
Garden, East Gosford, New South
Wales (Tel 2 4325 0056)

France
UNESCO Japanese Gardens,
Paris (Tel [0]1 45 68 10 00;
www.unesco.org)
Belgium
Hasselt Gardens, Hasselt
(Tel 0 11 23 95 40)
Germany
Bonn Japanese Garden
Freiburg Japanese Garden
Karlsruhe Japanese Garden
USA
Brooklyn Botanical Gardens,
New York (www.bbg.org)
Hakone Gardens, Saratoga,
California (Tel [408] 741-4994;
www.hakone.com)
Hammond Museum and
Japanese Stroll Garden, North
Salem, New York (Tel [914] 669-
5033; www.hammondmuseum.org)
Japanese Garden, Portland, Oregon
(www.japanesegarden.com)
Morikami Museum and Japanese
Gardens, Delray Beach, California
(www.morikami.org)
Canada
Nitobe Memorial Garden,
Vancouver (Tel [604] 822-6038)
New Zealand
Waitakere Japanese Garden,
Waitakere (Tel [09] 836 8000)

Japan
Daisen-in, Kyoto (Kita-ku,
Murasakino, Daitokuji-cho, Kyoto-shi)
Ginkaku-ji, Kyoto (Sakyo-ku,
Ginkakuji-cho, Kyoto-shi)
Joei-ji in, Yamaguchi, (Miyano-mura,
Yoshiki-gun)
Katsura Palace, Kyoto (get permis-
sion from the Imperial Park Agency)
Jiko-in, Nara
Joju-en, Kumamoto
Kenroku-en, Kanazawa
Koishikawa-Koraku-en, Tokyo
(Tel [0] 3-3811-3015)
Koraku-en, Okayama
Motsu-ji, Iwate
Raikyu-ji, Takahashi
Ryoan-ji, Kyoto (Ukyo-ku, Ryoanji,
Goryoshita-cho, Kyoto-shi)
Ryogen-in Zen Garden, Kyoto
(Ryogen-in Temple, Kyoto-shi)
Saiho-ji, Kyoto (write for permission
before visiting: Saiho-ji, Nishigyo-ku,
Kamigatani-cho, Matsuo, Kyoto)
Sanzen-in, Kyoto (Sakyo-ku, Ohara,
Raigoin-cho, Kyoto-shi)
Shisendo, Kyoto (Tel 075-781-
2954)
Shugakuin Palace, Kyoto (Sakyo-ku,
Shugakuin, Kyoto-shi)
Tôfuku-ji Hojo, Kyoto
(www.tofukuji.jp/english.html)

Index

Page numbers in *italics* refer to illustrations.

Acknowledgements and bibliography

Picture Acknowledgements

All photographs © Anness Publishing Ltd
except for the following:
Alamy Images: p59; **Charles Chesshire:** p4l, p4m;
p9m; p10m; p12; p16; p17t; p21t, p21br; p26;
p27; p28; p29b; p43t; p50; p55rb; p58; p66t;
p73l, p73r; p80; p82; p83r; p88r; p93t, p93m,
p93b; p96l; p101bl; p101br; p118l; p118r; p125l;
p133l; p141m, p141r; p142; p143l; p144l; p145r;
p149t; p155; **Jerry Harpur:** p4m; p9m; p17b;
p21bl; p21br; p25; p43b; p95; p111; p115;
p121tm; p127l; p137r; **Tadashi Kajiyana:** p30;
p31; p62t; p102; p105t; p131; p132r; p134;
p135l; p135m; p138.

Author's Acknowledgements

Thank you to all those who have helped enlighten
me on the many joys of Japanese gardens.

In Japan, I am eternally grateful to Venetia
Stanley-Smith for all her encouragement and
useful introductions, and to her husband Tadashi,
a few of whose photographs adorn the pages of
this book. Thanks to Masahiro Takaishi, creator
of the Japanese garden in Holland Park, who
showed me around and gave me lessons in

pruning. Also to Marc Keane who kindly included
me in his group of volunteers, weeding and
tidying the wonderful gardens of Hakusa-sonso.

To Gunter Nitschke for his stimulating hours
of discussions on the philosophies of Zen and
gardens over coffee in various places in Kyoto,
and for directing me to the most interesting sites.
A special thanks to Egami and his wife Hiromi
who took me to all kinds of wonderful places and
showed me some of the Ways of Tea, and the
intricacies of tea-house architecture.

Thanks to Alex Ramsay for suggesting that I
write this book and for a wonderful two weeks
in Kyoto, the fruits of which are evident in his
fabulous photographs. Thanks, too, to my wife
Anne for her encouragement and Nicola
Kearton for casting her eye over my first
draft. Finally thanks to my editor at Anness,
Caroline Davison, who listened patiently to
my persistent ideas of how I felt Japanese
gardens should be presented to those of us in
the West, and who helped to find the right
balance for the book.

To those who kindly opened their gardens to us:
a personal thanks from Alex and Charles to Kazuo
Tamura of Tatsumura Silk company for his garden
of Syoko-ho-en; Joho Ozeki for his hospitality at
the Jiko-in Zen Temple in Nara; Venetia Stanley-
Smith for introducing us to the private gardens of
Ohara and to the kind owners of those gardens;
and to the other temples and gardens in Japan
who kindly gave us permission to take
photographs: Byodo-in, Hakusa sonso, the Heian
Shrine, Honen-in, Hosen-in, Isui-en, Kinkaku-ji,
Koetsu-ji, Konchi-in, Koto-in, Murin-an, Nanzen-ji,
Nijo Castle, Ryoan-ji, Ryogen-in, Sanzen-in,
Shoden-ji, Tenju-an, Tofuku-Ji and Toji-in.

Bibliography

All the following are excellent references to gain
a broader view of Japanese gardens and the
background culture:

Conder, Josiah, *Japanese Gardens: An Illustrated
Guide to their Design and History*, orig.
written in 1893, reprinted 1964 by Dover
Publications Inc.

Keane, Marc P, *Japanese Garden Design*,
Tuttle 1996

Keswick, Maggie, *The Chinese Garden*, orig.
published by St Martins Press, republished by
Frances Lincoln 2003

Kuck, Lorraine, *The World of the Japanese
Garden*, Weatherhill 1968, repr. 1980

Nitschke, Gunter, *Japanese Gardens*, Taschen 1991

Shikibu, Murasaki, *The Tale of Genji*, translated by
Royall Tyler, Penguin 2001

Shonagon, Sei, *The Pillow Book*, translated by
Ivan Morris, Penguin 1967

Takei, Jiro, and Keane, Marc P, *Sakuteiki: Visions of
the Japanese Garden*, Tuttle 2001

Yoshikawa, Isao, *Japanese Stone Gardens*,
Graphic Shia 1992